HOOD'S LEGACY

NIXIE TAVERNER

By the same Author

A TORCH AMONG TAPERS

D0943486

HOOD'S LEGACY

First published by Bernard Durnford Publishing
The Old Museum, Bramber, West Sussex
BN44 3WE England.
2001

© Nixie Taverner 2001
All rights reserved

This book is sold subject to the condition that
it shall not, by way of trade or otherwise, be lent,
re-sold, hired out, or otherwise circulated without
the publisher's prior consent in any form
of binding or cover other than that in which it is
published and without a similar condition
being imposed on the subsequent purchaser.

A catalogue record of this book
is available from the British Library

ISBN 0 9535670 4 4

Format, design and cover by StewART

Printed and bound by, Antony Rowe Ltd

HOOD'S LEGACY

Nixie Taverner

Published by

Bernard Durnford Publishing

Hood's Legacy

CONTENTS

PUBLISHERS NOTE: Some of the photographic originals within this book have been included for their historical and sentimental value. Whilst every effort has been made, some of the original material prohibits good quality reproduction.

Hood's Legacy

Over the years, there have been many books written about Hood both before and after her loss.

Now, here is one which is very different.

This book centres mainly on the lives and memories of those still with us, who served with her and continue to cherish fond memories of that experience.

The Roll of Honour and a 'Memorial Gallery' are also included to help honour the lives of those who perished with her.

I congratulate Nixie on her stalwart efforts on behalf of 'our lady' both from myself and the Hood Association and wish the book the success it deserves.

Ted Briggs

Ted Briggs

ACKNOWLEDGEMENTS

I am greatly indebted to Ted Briggs, President of the Hood Association, for use of all the Association archives, to the Officers of the Committee for their help and support and also to the many Association members who have kindly contributed their memories of serving in the Mighty Hood.

My gratitude to Paul Bevand is also considerable both for the information he has accessed through the Hood Website (www.hmshood.com) and for the unfailing help he has given me in various ways, especially as a conscientious proof-reader.

My thanks are also due to my son John who kindly installed a PC for me (and patiently steered his mother through the traumatic early stages of acquiring basic 'computer literacy'); to my ever-supportive family for their continuing help and encouragement and to several friends, including Lorry Tait and Claire Spraggs for their professional help at the final stages of MS and disk assembly.

Due to the 'splendid 'network' embodied in the Hood Website first initiated by Frank Allen and then extended and maintained by Paul Bevand in the U.K., many valuable contacts have been established throughout the world. These contacts have reinforced the respect and affection Hood still commands sixty years after her catastrophic sinking. They have also resulted in a remarkable collection of memorabilia kindly donated by the relatives of many of the Hood casualties.

Additionally, Paul's widespread Press appeals for photographs to form a 'Memorial Gallery' of those who were lost, have elicited such a wide response, there was neither time nor space to include them all in 'Hood's Legacy'.

To do full justice to them, both in pictorial and written form, material is now being assembled for a further book which will be published at a later date in honour of Hood's many heroes.

Nixie Taverner

Hood's Legacy

This book is dedicated to the memory of HMS Hood
and the ten thousand men who served in her during
21 years; especially to the 1,418 who lost their lives
with her in 1941.

INTRODUCTION

HMS Hood - Even today, sixty years after her catastrophic sinking, the name has only to be mentioned by anyone, almost anywhere, for it to evoke an immediate response.

Known as 'The Mighty Hood' throughout the world, she was the largest, heaviest and fastest battle cruiser in the world during her time and she epitomised the power and supremacy of Britain's Navy.

The epitome of British Sea Power. The mighty Battlecruiser HMS Hood, in her day the World's largest Warship. Note the aircraft on 'B' turret.

She was also a truly beautiful ship, so the fact that she captured the hearts and minds of so many contemporaries throughout her life is understandable. The reason why that image is still cherished and her influence lives on, is embodied in the pages of this book.

A Brief Biography of Hood 1920 - 1941

Hood's origins can be traced to the early years of World War 1 and represented the outcome of an Admiralty decision concerning a proposed new class of battleships to complement ships of the Queen Elizabeth Class.

As the main purpose of the battleship was to fight gun duels with the heaviest enemy ships during naval action, speed was of secondary importance to armour protection. Ships of the new Elizabeth class were capable of 25 knots but actually limited to general Fleet speed of about 21 knots.

While battle cruisers lacked heavy armour they possessed tremendous speed that enabled them to outrun potential enemy battle fleets. Admiral of the Fleet Lord Fisher who had been the leading force behind the development of battle cruisers during the first decade of the 20th Century, believed that 'Speed is armour'. So when Admiral Jellicoe, C in C of the Home Fleet, reinforced this view during the Admiralty discussion of 1915, plans were finalised for the construction of four Admiral Class Battle Cruisers. Orders were then placed for work to begin on Hood with her proposed 'sister' ships Anson, Howe and Rodney, starting with Hood, on 1st September 1916.

This happened to be the period immediately after the ill-fated Battle of Jutland in which three Battle Cruisers, Indefatigable, Queen Mary and Invincible had been sunk. Admiral Beatty, C in C of the Battle Cruiser force, had been personally involved when his own Flagship, HMS Lion had narrowly avoided destruction from an enemy hit.

His outspoken comment to the Flag Captain, 'There's something wrong with our bloody ships today' no doubt reflected Admiralty misgivings as to the wisdom of laying down four new Battle Cruisers. Designs were amended and armour throughout the ships increased to reduce the possibility of similar disastrous losses being inflicted in the future.

Work on the new Battle Cruisers continued however and on Thursday 22nd August 1918, Hood was launched. The ceremony was performed by Lady Hood, widow of the Hon. Rear-Admiral Horace Hood who had been lost with his Flagship, Battle Cruiser Invincible at the Battle of Jutland.

Early in 1919, the Admiralty decided to cancel orders for Hood's three 'sisters'. Thus, Hood became unique as she alone would become the largest warship afloat. The fact that she could never be surpassed was due to two factors: the cancellation of her proposed 'sisters' construction and the Washington and London Naval

Treaties which placed strict limits on the size of warships built throughout the world during inter-war years.

Her Pedigree and "Vital statistics"

The first of Hood's three ancestors was named after Admiral, Viscount Samuel Hood (1724-1816) who was a fine Naval tactician in his time.

Built by John Brown and Company of Clydebank at an original cost of £6,025,000, her annual upkeep thereafter was £400,000. She was 860 feet long with a beam of 105 feet - in civilian terms, the equivalent of a third of a mile in length, or three football pitches. She had a displacement of 44,600 tons and a top speed of 32 knots. Her fuel consumption at full speed was three yards to the gallon and her four turbine engines delivered a total of 144,000 hp, each unit driving a 20 ton propeller.

Full speed 32 knots - 144,000 HP!

The total weight of her machinery was over 5,300 tons, but with pumps and ejectors for emptying water she could handle over 20,000 tons an hour. Her armour totalled 13,800 tons, was twelve inches thick 'on side' and she had protective bulges below for defence against torpedoes. She carried four 21-inch tube torpedoes above water and had eight 15 inch guns each weighing 100 tons, in a revolving turret of 900 tons.

There were also three steam and four motorboats, together with eleven sailing and pulling boats, which could accommodate a total of 759 men. In addition, there were enough Carley floats to carry the remainder of the ship's company.

Part of Hood's engine room, note ship's crest lower right foreground.

Within the ship there were 3,874 electric light fittings and 380 telephones. The total weight of electric cable, that could stretch for nearly 200 miles, was about two hundred tons.

No wonder then with such weighty equipment that Hood was the heaviest warship in the world. With her considerable displacement, she also proved quite a challenge in heavy seas. As many of her former 'residents' can testify, she had such a prodigious capacity for rolling and tossing, it is hardly surprising she is remembered as a 'wet ship '.

Life on Board

Catering for the ship's company

Running and maintaining a battle cruiser of such dimensions and complexity as the 'Mighty Hood' required a correspondingly large, well-trained crew. In fact, she was a floating home to a total company of over 1,400 men representing all ranks and a multiplicity of skills.

Providing for the physical fitness and general welfare of that vast 'family' required a high level of planning and organisation. Efficient catering for energy-sustaining meals was vital, especially when Hood was at sea for months. Some domestic 'statistics' indicate the nature of such requirements:

General provisions that had to be carried for four months, totalled about 320 tons and included one month's supply of refrigerated fresh meat.

There was a daily consumption of approximately 1,800lb. of bread, baked in the ship's galleys.

An average ship's breakfast in normal times would account for four sides of bacon, 300lb. of tomatoes, 100 gallons of tea, 100lb. of bread and 75lb. of butter.

There was also a canteen and bookshop on board where the sailors could buy extra nourishment for body and mind.

The installation of a sophisticated ventilation system whereby exhaust fans led direct to the open air, was of particular value to all the lower deck living area such as the seamen's quarters, 'heads', pantries and sculleries. Indeed, it was claimed at the time that 'A modern ship is, in many respects, a home of luxury compared with ships even ten or fifteen years old.'

Facilities for keeping fit

Like all warships in the British Navy, Hood's primary functions were defence of the shores, patrolling the seas and establishing a presence throughout the world. To fulfil this responsible role she had to maintain a state of readiness at all times. Whether 'At Watches' or 'Cruising Stations', all aboard had to be ready for 'Action Stations' at a moment's notice.

In view of the high level of alertness and physical stamina required of the crew, great emphasis was placed on Keep Fit activities of all kinds. Regular compulsory drill took place on the quarterdeck, conducted by Physical Training Instructors, for all those in training, especially the Boy sailors.

Although sports facilities were inevitably restricted by the ship's location and the lack of suitable space on board, boxing, wrestling and deck hockey were all popular. Played with quoits on the quarterdeck, the latter was strenuous and could be aggressive even if it was officially against the rules for sticks to be raised above shoulder level.

Hood alongside at Gibraltar 1935

Whenever Hood was in harbour, all possible use was made of every available facility for competitive land and water sports. Field games such as soccer and rugger were always popular while athletics and cross-country running were both widely encouraged, especially as they were relatively easy to organise in varied terrains. They also

15

provided suitable scope for team competitions between Hood's twenty departments, ranging from cooks to signalmen. Later, winning teams competed against those from other ships in the Fleet for the much-coveted Arbuthnot Trophy - often won by Hood.

Hood's soccer team enjoyed a 'friendly' game against a team from the German Pocket Battleship Admiral Graf Spee at Gibraltar during 1936.

Rifle shooting, another popular sport, could only be practised when Hood was in port, ideally at Portsmouth with its easy access to the Whale Island Gunnery school. Aquatic sports such as swimming, rowing and sailing, were also extensively enjoyed with Fleet Regattas as the focal point of competitive effort.

Entertainment

Even amidst such a plethora of compelling activity, time was also found for various chosen leisure pursuits. Card games like 'Solo' were a familiar feature of off-duty activity on the lower deck and although gambling was strictly forbidden, it appears that 'loop-holes' were found to counter the rule of 'No money on the table'. There was also a flourishing Seamen's Band in addition to the more ceremonial one of the Royal Marines while the Ship's Own Dramatic Society (known rather irreverently as the S.O.D's Opera), provided splendid scope for those with dramatic talent.

There seems little doubt that in accordance with time-honoured tradition, all Hood sailors enjoyed entertaining themselves and each other both ashore and afloat.

Medical Welfare

The medical care of the crew was furthered by the existence of a well-equipped Sick Bay. It resembled a miniature hospital, complete with an operating theatre, X-Ray facilities and all the most modern appliances of the time.

Hood's Sick Bay.

Provision for Spiritual Welfare

As in all ships, there was some provision for the sailors' spiritual welfare with a resident Church of England Chaplain on board. Unlike his Army and Air Force counterparts, he never wore uniform and was as much at home on the mess deck as in the ward-room. He was readily available for advice and conducted services whenever suitable occasions arose.

Sunday was always a special day when Divisions were held on the quarterdeck for the entire ship's company and included a relevant, short Service with a Hymn and prayer or two.

Hood's simple Chapel for quiet prayer and meditation.

Hood was one of the few ships that possessed a Chapel. It was situated aft, just below the quarterdeck and was graced by original Sanctuary panelling and Communion rails made on board by the ship's Carpenters.

A Sunday Communion Service was held there at 8 a.m. whenever Hood was in harbour but as there was only room for twelve, attendance was restricted to a few. They usually represented a cross section of ranks from Captain to 'boys' and are fondly remembered by several old 'Hoods' such as Reverend Ron Paterson (the Hood Association Padré). He was 'Chapel Sweeper' to the Chaplain, J.C. Waters during the 1933-1936 Commission and says he owes a lot to his influence - as well as to Commander Rory O'Conor. Ron also remembers that as part of his Chapel duties, he had to lock away the Communion wine at the end of each Service, in case it went astray.

On a more solemn note, he maintains that from his experience, sailors cannot easily be regular Churchgoers but many have a strong and abiding faith.

They that go down to the sea in ships

and occupy their business in great waters,

These men see the works of the Lord

And his wonders in the deep.

(Psalm 107 23-24)

Early in her career Hood became known as 'Pride of the Navy' across the world owing to her fine appearance and the number of courtesy visits she made between the wars.

HOOD'S: TIME-LINE

Outline Log From January 1920 - 24 May 1941

1920
Jan- May
During the 18 months following her launching, Hood spent a few months at Rosyth where she underwent completion and trials. She was commissioned on 29 March by Captain Wilfred Tomkinson with a crew of 967.

While en route for Plymouth, she was assigned as Flagship, Battle Cruiser Squadron on 18 May when Rear-Admiral Sir Roger Keyes became the first Admiral to fly his flag from Hood as Commander of the Battle Cruiser Squadron.

June
With Tiger and 9 destroyers, she sailed on her first 'Goodwill Cruise' to Scandinavia. Her draught was too great for docking at Stockholm but she had several royal visitors; the King of Sweden at Nynashamm, The King of Denmark at Copenhagen and the King of Norway at both Kioge Bay and Christiana.

July - Aug
For the next two months, Hood was in Scottish waters, at Scapa Flow, Cromarty, Dunbar and Rosyth. While at Lamlash, she won the Battle Cruiser Regatta - one of many such achievements.

Sept - Dec
The autumn was spent off the S.W. coast of England with several short cruises, various exercises and some weeks in port at Penzance, Portland and Devonport.

1921

Jan - Mar
Hood remained in the West Country with visits to Falmouth, in addition to Devonport and Portland, until 21 January when she left for a Spring cruise to Gibraltar and the Iberian Peninsula. At the end of March she returned once more to Devonport where command was taken by Captain Geoffrey Mackworth, known as the 'least-loved skipper'. He evidently clocked up a record number of 'corrections' levelled at officers, several relating to 'the demon drink'. They then returned to Gibraltar for the rest of the year.

Jan - Apr
In company with the 1st Battle Squadron under the flag of Rear-Admiral Sir Walter Cowan, Hood had numerous short cruises, drills and trials including dummy torpedo 'strikes' which she survived unscathed.

April-May
Following a spell at familiar West Country ports, she went to Rosyth where Scottish members of the crew were given 2 weeks leave while those remaining on board cleaned, repaired and painted the ship.

May -June
Back at Devonport again, they experienced some unusual events. Leave was given to both watches, a crewman was sent to prison and they fired salutes for a royal visitor, the Prince of Wales. Later in June, more routine exercises were carried out such as submarine attack, gunnery practice, sub-calibre and torpedo firing.

July

Still based in home waters, Hood extended her area of influence to Weymouth and Torbay where King George V came aboard to inspect the ship.

August

In mid-August, she went back to Gibraltar for another Summer cruise. Sadly, while en route for St. Vincent, a boy sailor, Alfred Field, went missing - presumed overboard/drowned and was later the subject of a Court of Enquiry.

Sept - Oct

Hood's first extensive tour was to Rio de Janeiro where she represented Great Britain at Brazil's independence celebrations. The ship's brief stop at the Equator, provided for many, a first experience of the Crossing the Line ceremony - so special to sailors.

Nov

While at Rio, members of the crew participated in a 'mini Olympics' against those from other Navies including Argentina, Brazil, Mexico and the U.S.A. Hood demonstrated her sports prowess with 5 boxers, three of whom won their fights against the American team.

Following prestigious visits to Santos, Trinidad, Barbados and St. Lucia, she left for Las Palmas, stopping at Dominica for a Memorial Service in memory of young Alfred Field.

On return to Europe, they went to Gibraltar for the rest of the month. While there, she conducted tours for dignitaries such as the Governor and Vice-Admiral of Gibraltar, participated in a Squadron Regatta and carried out general cleaning and maintenance work.

Dec

Back at Devonport, Hood stayed in situ until the end of the year for cleaning, provisioning and welcome spells of leave for both Watches.

1923

Jan - May

Hood's first assignment for the New Year was to Gibraltar with the Atlantic Fleet for an extensive range of exercises and maintenance with short cruises to Malaga, Cartagena and Valencia. Regrettably, another death occurred to P.O. Thomas Martin Broad due to an acute haemorrhage of the pancreas.

While based at Gibraltar, the ship's company took part in a March past/review for the Rear Admiral commanding the Battle Cruiser Squadron and the C in C Home Fleet. During May, Captain John Knowles Im Thurn assumed command of Hood.

July
A second short cruise to Scandinavia, with Repulse and Snapdragon following a refit at Devonport in preparation for the world cruise.

Hood's World Cruise

Vice-Admiral Sir Frederick Lawrence Field, KCB, CMG., Admiral Commanding the 'Cruise of the Special Squadron'.

Captain John Knowles Im Thurn, CBE., Captain of Hood and Chief Staff Officer during the 'Cruise of the Special Squadron'.

Nov
27 November marked the start of Hood's memorable Round the World Cruise. Known officially as the 'Cruise of the Special Squadron', it was dubbed 'The booze cruise' by the sailors, and

mainly 'Empire Cruise' by the Press. Whatever her appellation, she was the centre piece of this prestigious tour - a public relations exercise that focused on the British Empire and served as a reminder that Britannia still 'ruled the waves' and encouraged other nations in the Empire to support the Royal Navy.

Away for nearly a year, the Squadron visited numerous countries throughout the year and covered a distance of 38,152 miles. During the cruise over one million people visited the Squadron with a total of 752,000 visiting Hood alone.

Other vessels participating in the Cruise were Battle Cruiser Repulse, and light cruisers Delhi, Dauntless, Danae, Dragon and Dunedin, joined by H.M.A.S. Adelaide in Australia.

Cruise Itinerary

Africa and the Indian Ocean

Dec 8-13
Their first port of call was to Freetown, Sierra Leone and then, en route for Cape Town, they enjoyed another Crossing the Line ceremony on the 14th December.

Dec 22-
2 Jan 1924
While at Cape Town, they received numerous visitors and held a Squadron Ball.

Dec 28 -31
The ship re-fuelled and re-provisioned and both Watches enjoyed shore leave.

1924
Jan 2-6
They paid brief calls at Mossell Bay, then East London and Durban.

Jan 6-12
En route to Zanzibar, the ship was fully cleaned and sea-boat crews thoroughly exercised.

Jan 12-17
While at Zanzibar, they received Sultan Sayyad Khaifa Ben Harud and many other visitors. A ceremonial 'march past' was also conducted ashore.

Jan 17-26
On the way to Trincomalee, Ceylon (Sri Lanka), the usual cleaning and sea-boat exercises were followed by gunnery practise.

Jan 26-31
Many visitors were also received while they were at Trincomalee.

Jan 31
04 Feb
En route to Port Swettenham, Kuala Lumpur, Malaya, various standard exercises included gunnery and torpedo control parties.

Feb 4-9
At Port Swettenham, gun salutes were fired for the Sultans of Perak, Pehang and Negri Sembilan. Many sailors were allowed ashore for 'exercises' but difficulties arose due to the extreme heat and water contaminated by salt. Sadly, malaria caused considerable suffering and the death of Able Seaman Walter Benger who was buried in a local cemetery.

Feb 9-10
Their next short trip was from Port Swettenham to Singapore.

Feb 11-17
While there, the ship was opened to visitors and gun salutes were fired for Admiral Sir A.L. Lebeson and Major General Sir N. Malcolm. On the way to Australia in late February, they encountered very heavy seas.

Feb 17-1 March
They reached calmer waters at Fremantle, Perth, Western Australia and then went to Albany where the first colony was established in 1827.

Mar 10-14
Later, while at Adelaide, the Squadron had over 69,000 visitors.

Hood arrives at Fremantle, Western Australia

*Adelaide, South Australia where the 'Special Squadron'
welcomed 69,000 visitors.*

Mar 17-24

Sadly, at Melbourne, another death occurred when Signal
Boatswain Albert Punshon who had played King Neptune in the
Crossing the Line Ceremony, had a sudden, fatal heart attack.

Mar 26-
Their next port of call was Hobart Bay where they stayed for two days until 3 April going to Jervis Bay, New South Wales on 5th April

'Top Brass' go ashore at Sydney, New South Wales.

April 9-20
During a longer and probably, quite recuperative stay at Sydney, HMS Dunedin transferred to the New Zealand Navy.

April 24 - 8 May
They also remained for over two weeks at Wellington, New Zealand.

May 10-18
Their last visit 'Down under' was to Auckland. While in New Zealand Admiral Jellicoe, Governor General at the time, was on board.

Hood arrives in New Zealand.

Admiral of the Fleet, Lord Jellicoe,
Governor General of New Zealand visits
Hood.

Across the Pacific to North America

May 22-27
During a pleasant crossing of the Pacific Ocean, they paused at Suva, Fiji and then called at Apia, Western Samoa.

June 6-12
Their visit to Honolulu was evidently somewhat blighted by the American 'Prohibition' laws and enforced sobriety ashore!

June 20-25
A longer stay at Victoria Island, British Columbia (Canada), was more convivial and then followed by a stay at Vancouver before they left Canada.

July 7-11
After a few days at San Francisco, California, they left the U.S.A. and the First Light Cruiser Squadron was detached to visit South America.

Central America/Caribbean

July 23-24
Travelling through the Panama Canal proved an extremely tight fit with tolls that totalled 22,390.50 dollars.

Hood traversing the Panama Canal - a tight squeeze for a Mighty Ship.

Homeward bound from the Panama Canal.

July 26
Following their arrival at Kingston, Jamaica, they remained for several days until June 30 leaving for Eastern Canada.

Eastern Canada

August
They enjoyed a welcome, longer stay at Halifax, Nova Scotia before leaving for Quebec.

Aug 19 - Sept 1
After an even longer stay at Quebec, their penultimate call was Topsail Bay, St. John's, Newfoundland.

Sept 6-21
The final few weeks in the 'New World' marked the end of Hood's momentous and memorable World Cruise.

Sept -Oct
On their return to Devonport at the end of September - following an Atlantic crossing, they linked up with the First Light Cruiser Squadron off The Lizard.

October - December
Their last port of call for the year was Devonport for an extensive overhaul.

1925

January
Assigned as Flagship of the Battle Cruiser Squadron, Atlantic Fleet, Hood visited Lisbon, Portugal, as a goodwill representative of Vasco Da Gama Day.

February- March
They were once more at Gibraltar for their annual Spring Cruise that included trips to various Spanish ports such as Palma de Majorca.

April
When they returned to Devonport, Rear-Admiral Sir Cyril Fuller replaced Vice-Admiral Sir Frederick Field and Captain Harold Owen Reinold took over command.

May -July
Their next cruise was to Portree, Isle of Skye and Portrash, followed by a visit to Lamlash on Arran.

July - August
Their return to southern waters brought them back to Weymouth, Devonport and Portland for two months.

Sept - December
This was followed by a few months in equally familiar Scottish waters at Invergordon and a minor refit at Rosyth.

1926

January - March
Hood returned to southern waters again, this time to Portsmouth where she stayed for a few months until the effects of the post-war Depression took her back north.

The coveted 'Rodman Cup' won by Hood in 1926.

March - May
After repairs at Rosyth, she was assigned to guard the Princess Docks near Glasgow during the General Strike.

Sept - December
Hood remained at Invergordon for the rest of the year.

1927
January - March
Back to the Mediterranean again, they visited Gibraltar once more and also Palma

May - July
While they were on patrol duty at Cromarty, Rear-Admiral Sir Frederick Dreyer replaced Admiral Sir Cyril Fuller and Captain Wilfred French assumed command of Hood.

Then, for the rest of the year, they divided their time between English and Scottish Waters:

July -Aug   At Devonport

Sept- Nov   At Invergordon

Nov- Dec   At Devonport

1928
Jan - May
They were assigned to Battle Cruiser Squadron, Atlantic Fleet

1929
May -
Following the crew's pay-off at Portsmouth, Hood underwent such a prolonged refit, it continued for the whole of the following year and well into the next one.

1931
May
When re-commissioned, Hood was assigned as Flagship to the Battle Cruiser Squadron, Home Fleet.

June - July
Ready for action again, Hood and her new company 'worked up' off the South Coast. During a visit to Torbay, Admiral Wilfred Tomkinson who had been Hood's first Captain, took command of the Squadron and flew his flag over his old ship.

Sept
Having sailed north to Scottish waters, Hood became involved in the famous Invergordon Mutiny, largely because some of the crew supported the cut-in-pay protest that erupted in the Fleet. (It would seem that later findings ascribed some blame to Admiral Tomkinson for failing to deal severely with the insurgents possibly because he had some sympathy with them.)

1932
Jan - Feb
In the aftermath of all the Invergordon publicity and enquiries, Hood welcomed a therapeutic cruise to the West Indies. With Repulse and three cruisers, they called first at Madeira and then visited St.Vincent, Grenada, Barbados and Trinidad.

Feb - June
Back at Portsmouth, they had another refit before their next assignment - the 'Depression cruise' when they toured the East Coast in an effort to remind the depression-weary population of Britain's continuing greatness.

July - Aug
They then returned to Portsmouth where Admiral James assumed command of the Squadron for another trip north, to Rosyth, in November.

1933
The first part of the year was spent at Gibraltar with visits to Algiers and Tangiers.

March - May
Next, they went back to base at Portsmouth for yet another, but shorter refit, from 31st March to 10th May.

Aug.
The commission ended with the usual paying-off in readiness for the arrival of a new Captain and company.

Sept - Oct
The new company's first trip was to Rosyth for Autumn manoeuvres off Scotland. Then they participated in exercises near Invergordon where realistic rehearsals ashore for the Pirates of Penzance, gave rise to rumours of another mutiny!

Nov
The year ended with a refit.

1934
January
Exercises with the Mediterranean Fleet included visits to Madeira and Gibraltar.

March

In March, they visited Lagos, Nigeria and while there, took part in an Inter Port Regatta. When the President of the Portuguese Republic, Senor Carmona, visited the British Fleet anchored in the Bay, he paid them a glowing tribute. He said: 'It was a great pleasure for me to visit the splendid ship HMS Hood, the marvel of British shipbuilding. I was here able to admire the fine spirit of British sailors.'

May

Back at Portsmouth, shooting enthusiasts won the Port Rifle Trophy before Hood joined the Home Fleet for a Summer Cruise to Gibraltar.

June

They then returned to Plymouth before going north to Scapa and some Bombardment range practice at Loch Eriboll.

July

A more prolonged stay provided scope for shore activities such as Competitive Athletics that was won by a member of Hood's crew.

August

In August they went to Portsmouth for a spectacular Navy Week. Opened officially by Lord Beatty, it attracted a record number of visitors with Hood as the 'star'. Admiral Sir Sidney Bailey took command of the Squadron and raised his flag.

Sept

Apart from a short period of exercises in the Hull area, they remained at Portsmouth until the end of the year with welcome spells of leave.

1935

January

Early in January, during Fleet exercises off the coast of Spain, an improbable collision occurred between Hood and Renown. There was no injury to personnel but slight structural damage to both ships, extensive publicity and investigation, culminating in a Court Martial.

Rocket display by the Fleet during Jubilee celebrations.

March
By late March when all the controversy had died down, Hood was back at Gibraltar long enough for the crew to enjoy some Regatta training before returning to Portsmouth in time for some Easter leave.

July
While in their home port for a few months, more time could be given to various sporting activities. They resulted in several more trophies and culminated in a memorable Jubilee Review when George V reviewed the Fleet.

August
Another Navy Week attracted a record attendance of 103,640 visitors to Hood and the first large scale model of the ship was on show. It featured every aspect of her structure and life on board, including a replica of Commander Rory O'Conor's dog, Judy

Sept- Nov
Following their return to Gibraltar, their stay was extended until June the subsequent year, due to the volatile international situation arising from Mussolini's invasion of Abyssinia.

1936

During May, the deposed Emperor, Haile Selassie, visited Hood and was received with great sympathy.

July

Hood was back at Portsmouth at the start of the Spanish Civil War on 18 July for a refit.

Oct

When she left port in October, gravel was sucked into her condensers and she was forced to return for repair. By mid-October, she was able to fulfil her next mission and sail for Malta.

Nov

On 28 November, Admiral Geoffrey Blake raised his flag over Hood.

Dec

During December, Hood and Repulse operated out of Gibraltar to patrol the Spanish coast and protect British shipping in the area.

1937

Spring

As the Spanish Civil War escalated, Fascist states Germany and Italy began exporting equipment openly to Franco's forces.

April 6

The first confrontation between Nationalist (pro-Franco) forces and British peace-keepers occurred when a Spanish merchant ship bound for Bilbao with a cargo of food, was stopped by Nationalist ships and had to be escorted to safety by British destroyers.

April 10

Hood was sent to Bilbao to provide a cautionary presence and a few days later extended her patrol area to the French coast at La Rochelle.

23

Hood's first direct encounter took place when three steamers carrying supplies from France were stopped by Franco's ships and had to be 'convoyed' to safety under cover of her guns.

May

By way of contrast, she returned to Portsmouth for the Coronation Review of King George V1.

June

Next, they rejoined the Mediterranean Fleet and were based at Malta with Repulse, Glorious and the repair ship Resource.

During the next two months, Hood resumed the role of protecting British and neutral shipping from piracy, including an increased threat from Italian submarines. The area extended to Barcelona, Valencia and Majorca. During this period, Admiral Blake suffered two serious heart attacks and was replaced by Admiral Cunningham who took over officially on July 15th.

Aug

Captain HTC 'Hookey' Walker assumed command of the ship and 20 they returned to Malta and continued 'on the alert' until the end of the year. During November, they received the French Naval C in C, Admiral Abriel.

1938

Jan 5 -Feb

Leaving Malta, they went first to Palma de Majorca and then remained in Spanish waters on patrol between Barcelona and Valencia until early February when they returned to Malta once more for the next month.

Mar- April

For the next month they continued on patrol in Spanish waters.

April

They arrived at Golfe Juan, France for a welcome period of 'R and R' and then further patrol assignments before returning to Malta.

May 16--June 22

Refit at Malta.

Aug

Admiral Sir Geoffrey Layton raised his Command flag on Hood on 22nd August before a cruise to Gibraltar.

Sept

They arrived at Gibraltar on 20th September but had to disperse on 28th in case hostilities with Germany erupted.

Nov

Their last trip for the year was to Pariatorio, Malta on 24 November for the use of dry dock facilities.

1939

Jan

Hood left Malta on 10 January and returned to Portsmouth for a long refit on the 18th.

Feb- Aug 13

They remained in Portsmouth for six months for another refit, after which, Captain Irvine Glenney took command and Admiral William J.Whitworth transferred his flag to Hood.

Aug 31

Under her new command, Hood sailed for Scapa Flow, as Flagship of the Battle Cruiser squadron, Home Fleet, in company with the battle cruisers Repulse and Renown. They were at sea, on patrol, from 20 - 28 August, between N. Scotland and Norway.

Sept 1

Pending the possible commencement of hostilities with Germany, they left Scapa Flow for their first on-the-verge-of-war assignment - covering the Iceland-Faroes Pass for any potential break-out attempts by the 'Kriegsmarine Atlantic'

Sept 3

When the start of World War 2 was announced, Hood returned at once to her Scapa Flow base for immediate 'Action Stations'.

5

Their first encounter with the enemy was a near miss from a torpedo fired by a German U-boat.

8 - 12

They then returned to the Iceland-Faroes pass to prevent German ships entering Atlantic shipping lanes, together with Renown, the cruisers Belfast and Edinburgh and four destroyers.

22- 24

While on patrol in the North Sea, escort ships spotted a U-boat and mine but had no active engagement.

26

In company with Renown, a number of cruisers and destroyers, Hood effected the rescue of Spearfish, a damaged submarine from the Horns Reef/Dogger Bank area off Denmark. On their return trip, the group was attacked by Luftwaffe bombers and Hood was struck by a bomb. Fortunately, it glanced off her side on the port quarter and detonated in the sea so there was no serious damage.

Oct 8

This was a very special day for all the ship's company because they were visited by the First Lord of the Admiralty, the famous Winston Churchill. On the same day, Hood, Repulse plus cruisers, Aurora and Sheffield were ordered to cover the northern approaches to Bergen, Norway. Their objective was to intercept the battlecruiser Gneisenau and heavy cruiser Koln but the Kriegsmarine chose to retreat once more.

10

They returned to Loch Ewe briefly, then departed to join with Nelson, Rodney, Furious, Aurora, Belfast and 9 destroyers to intercept potential German shipping in the Denmark Strait.

30

Another near miss! Hood, Nelson and Rodney set out to escort an iron ore convoy from Narvik, Norway to the UK, when the group was unknowingly attacked by U-boat U56 off Orkney Islands. 3 torpedoes were launched at Nelson, 1 missed completely, but the others struck the ship. Fortunately, neither detonated.

Nov

It was probably a relief to return to home waters and operate out of Plymouth.

21

Scharnhorst and Gneisenau were detected attempting to break-out into the North Atlantic. Hood and a group of destroyers combined forces, successfully, with elements of the French Navy under the command of French Vice Admiral Gensoul. Their next objective was to patrol the area south of Iceland and hopefully, intercept the raiders. When the Germans once again chose to retreat to home waters, Hood returned to her Plymouth base where they remained until early December.

Dec 2

Once more they returned to northern waters and temporarily operated out of Loch Ewe while Scapa Flow was undergoing defensive improvements. In mid-December when the first convoy of troops returned from Canada, escorted by Furious, Repulse, Emerald, Hunter and Hyperion, Hood was required to supplement them with Barham and Warspite.

1940

Jan-Feb

During the first two months, they were involved with intensive patrol duties out of Greenock.

Mar 2 - 8

Their next assignment was to protect a convoy from Norway with Valiant and six destroyers. Having returned to Scapa Flow, Hood was visited again by Winston Churchill - transferred from Rodney who was unable to enter harbour due to mines dropped by the Luftwaffe. Later in March they were in the far north again, operating patrols out of the Shetlands

29

There was a necessary break in their active duties for a major refit that took place at Devonport that lasted for nearly two months and involved a number of major modifications.

April

Hood was unable to take an active part in the operation Primrose attempt to relieve Andalsnes Norway because she was undergoing her long refit but she sent 250 Marines and a Howitzer to join the ships going from Scotland.

May

Late in May, it was found necessary for the ship to visit Liverpool to use the Gladstone dry dock for the underwater sections of the ship to be inspected, repaired and painted.

June

In June she returned to convoy duty and escorted the famous Convoy US3 with liners Andes, Aquitania, Empress of Britain, Empress of Canada, Mauretania and Queen Mary on the last stages of a perilous journey to Greenock.

8

With Ark Royal,Valiant, Resolution, Arethusa, Enterprise and destroyers of the 8th and 13th Flotillas, Hood was assigned to the Cagliari Air Base, Italy, to divert attention away from two convoys and a planned strike against forces near Calabria.

18 - 23

Hood had a change of scene when she was ordered to join Ark Royal for a trip to Gibraltar where they formed the core of the new Force H.

25

It was a sad day for France - after the historic evacuation of Dunkirk - when Marshall Petain signed an armistice with Germany. Concerned that the French Fleet might fall into the hands of the enemy, Britain was impelled to deliver an ultimatum whereby they either agreed to support the allied cause or be sunk in neutral ports.

30

The Admiral in charge of Force H, Sir James Somerville, transferred his command flag to Hood.

July 3

Forced to implement their ultimatum, Hood with Ark Royal, Valiant, Resolution, Arethusa, Enterprise and eleven destroyers, attacked the French Fleet at Oran. Described by a witness as 'shooting fish in a barrel', the French suffered heavy losses with four ships put 'out of commission' and 1,300 men killed. British ships and personnel sustained no casualties.

4

When they returned to Gibraltar, they were unsuccessfully attacked by French Air Force bombers without any hits or injuries.

9

Another air attack on Force H by Regia Aeronautica bombers caused several near misses but not serious damage. The Cagliari mission had to be aborted after some success as both convoys arrived safely and Regia Marina forces were driven from Calabria.

31

The next assignment for Hood, Valiant, Enterprise and nine destroyers was to escort carriers Ark Royal 111 and Argus on missions deep into the Mediterranean. Argus launched 12 Hawker Hurricanes, bound for Malta, from Cape Bon while Ark Royal's Swordfish successfully attacked The Cagliari Air Base.

Aug

Their first experience of enemy action at the beginning of the month was an unsuccessful attack by Savoia bombers of the Regia Aeronautica.

8

They then returned to Gibraltar for a few days before going up to Scapa Flow where Admiral Sir William Whitworth returned to command from Hood.

By mid August they were at Rosyth for a replacement of 'A' turret's left 15in. gun and then returned once more to Scapa.

Sept 13

Hood, Nelson, Rodney, Bonaventure, Naiad, Cairo and seven destroyers returned to patrol off Rosyth.

28

They were dispatched to intercept a German convoy and cruiser reported in the vicinity of Stavanger, Norway but after the mission was aborted, they returned to Scapa.

Oct 15

Hood was then assigned to cover carrier Furious and cruisers Berwick and Norfolk who were scheduled to launch an airstrike against the enemy at Tromso, Norway but due to bad weather, Hood had to be re-routed to Scapa.

Nov 5 - 10
Hood and Repulse, with 3 cruisers and 15 destroyers, covered approaches to Brest and Lorient, France in an attempt to catch the pocket battleship Admiral Scheer. They then returned to Scapa.

23
Their next assignment was to provide cover for mine-laying operations north of the Denmark Strait.

Dec 24 - 29
Next, they were assigned with the cruiser Edinburgh and 4 destroyers to patrol the Iceland-Faroes Pass in case the enemy cruiser Admiral Hipper should attempt a break-through. But, as usual, there was no sign of the Germans.

1941
Jan 1 - 2
With Scapa Flow as her base, Hood's first assignment for the year was to provide escort for a mine-laying operation near the Faroes. Fortunately, when an enemy mine was encountered by a paravane off Dunnet Head, it was cleared quite easily.

Mar 13 - 15
During a minor refit at Rosyth, various functional modifications were effected including the replacement of steam picket boats with 35ft. motor launches. Captain Ralph Kerr had assumed command on 15th Feb and King George V1, with Churchill, had inspected the ship on 6th March.

18
Hood eventually left Rosyth for Scapa where she joined Queen Elizabeth and Nelson. Their objective was to find and attack Scharnhorst and Gneisenau but when the Germans diverted their ships to Brest to avoid any risks, Hood and her companions returned to base.

April 21
With Kenya and a small destroyer screen, Hood was sent to intercept the new Kriegsmarine battleship - the pride of the German Navy - but when on patrol off Iceland, they discovered that instead of attempting to enter the Atlantic, the German battleship had gone to Gotenhafen (Gydnia), Poland.

The 'Great Lady' puts to sea..........

May 5
The whole day was devoted to gunnery practice.

8
Admiral Lancelot E. Holland, the new Commander of the Battle Cruiser Squadron and Second-in-Command of the Home Fleet, raised his Flag over Hood.

No-one could possibly have imagined that Hood's next assignment would be her last.

22

She was sent with the new battleship Prince of Wales and destroyers Acates, Antelope, Anthony, Echo, Electra and Icarus, to cover the Denmark Strait in case Bismarck and the accompanying heavy cruiser Prince Eugen should attempt a break-out in the Atlantic.

Two days later, the adversaries 'engaged' with devastating results.

24

Just before 6 am. Hood went into battle for the last time. In company with the Prince of Wales, she engaged Bismarck and the heavy Cruiser Prince Eugen. Minutes later, Hood was struck by a deep hit from Bismarck that caused a massive fire and a colossal explosion. Within minutes, she broke apart and sank deep into Arctic waters. So ended 21 years of her short but spectacular life and with her, the lives of practically all her crew of 1,421 men.

Miraculously, there were three survivors who had been blown clear of the stricken ship and were eventually picked up. Of the three, Ordinary Signalman Ted Briggs, Midshipman William Dundas and Able Seaman Robert Tilburn, only one - the intrepid Ted Briggs is still living today. He retired from the Navy in 1973 after thirty two years of service and is President of the flourishing Hood Association.

The Royal Naval War Memorial, Southsea,
Lt. A.E. Briggs, MBE, RN, (Rtd)
Survivor of Hood, attending the Remembrance Service,
Sunday 8th November 1987.

"With Favouring Winds"

TO LOST SAILORS

HMS Hood - May 1941

Untroubled by the tumult of the sea,
So peacefully you rest beneath the deep,
For years unseen and yet remembered still
Locked in our hearts where none can do you ill
Or spoil the memory of lives so bravely spent;
Young lives, too soon by savage war curtailed,
Bright youth, extinguished in the battle's roar;
So long apart and yet we still recall
Unsparing courage, model to us all,
And we who follow on must never fail
To keep in mind the anguish and the pain
Of loved ones, left to mourn upon the shore.
Peace must be our aim for evermore
Lest your great sacrifice be made in vain.

By Bee Kenchington

CHAPTER ONE

Hood Association Highlights

The Hood Association owes its inception to a Weymouth resident, Fred White. He was evidently motivated by the proximity of the Portland base and contact with a group of ex-Hoods, including two of the three survivors, Robert Tilburn and William Dundas. The third, the intrepid Lieutenant Ted Briggs was the Association's first President and, happily, he continues to thrive and still officiates.

Fred White's first Newsletter in 1975 marked the official launch of the Association although it had been formed earlier - judging by his exhortation to Members:

'This is the first Newsletter of the Association and may it long continue. It will only if you can supply me with material to keep it interesting - that I'm sure you will want to do and can do..'

He had so much faith in the venture that he paid for the printing and distribution of the first issue himself on condition that members observed his stricture, continued to keep in touch and contribute material.

In response to his request for reminiscences from shipmates, he recorded the following: Shipmate Doug. Woodward of Dorchester wrote that 'In January 1935 when men were recalled from pubs, cinemas and the Regent Dance Hall, Weymouth, Hood left Portland in a force 8 gale.' Although all the mess-decks were awash, she maintained a steady 29 knots and by reaching Gibraltar in just over 38 hours, established a record.

Shipmate Allen of Maiden Newton, Dorchester, recalled that when Hood carried out a speed trial across Weymouth Bay, the wash carried away deck chairs and everything else mobile on the beach.

Shipmate Ivor Smith of Weymouth was in Hood when she was 'rammed by Renown'; he served later in Malaya during the War but claimed that of all the ships he experienced, Hood was quite the happiest.

Fred himself remembered the thunderous roar of guns when they put to sea 'for a shoot' and how and when they 'fell in' even on Christmas Day, the Commander ordered 'Carry on and scrub decks' as usual but added, as an afterthought, 'Merry Christmas'.

The second Newsletter in the same year, also contained a graphic description of Hood at sea: 'She always presented a terrifying sight when at speed on the high seas with her quarterdeck awash and her funnels rumbling like thunder as they expanded with the heat, while emitting dense clouds of oily smoke'. Some recalled that the deep rumble and vibrations of Hood's guns in Portland Bay would even shatter the school windows at the Dorset village of Langton Herring unless they were left open!

Hood in heavy seas.

In a masterly summary of his three years in Hood from 1933 - 1936 as a young Jixer, the diarist wrote: ' What a ship! Efficient - Fast - Happy - Beautiful lines - Good at sport - Football - Running - Good at everything - Cock of the Fleet!'

In the third Newsletter, during 1976, Fred was pleased to report that the Standard fund was building up well and should be ready in time for their Memorial Service and that a Hood tie was already available, for the princely sum of £1.45. It was agreed that the Association year should run, most appropriately, from 24 May.

The rest of the letter was devoted to a poignant account of Hood's last days recalled by the Association President Ted Briggs.

Sea-faring has always inspired a great deal of memorable poetry of which the following 'Epitaph to stricken comrades' is a moving example:

We that survive perchance may end our days
In some employment meriting no praise.
They have outlived this fear and their brave ends
Will ever be an honour to their friends.

Phineas James, Shipmaster

The fourth Newsletter dated 1977, was packed with information giving details of Committee Officers both in this country and from overseas Branches in Canada, Malta, New Zealand, South Africa and N.A.T.O.

During a meeting held in Fareham during July, members' comments were invited on the proposed liaison with the Bismarck Association in Germany.

It is appropriate that one of the two reminiscences that followed, featured the memories of R.C. Bragg from Capetown, South Africa.

He joined Hood in 1923 during her first Commission and said that when he sat between the two 15" guns in 'A' turret and heard the first salvo, he thought: 'The end of the world had come'! Twenty

Hood's 15 inch guns in action.

years later, when serving in HMS Newcastle, during another visit to Cape Town, he met his second wife and enjoyed many happy years of marriage.

Windy Breeze also recalled his early days aboard Hood as Blue Marine and explained how he acquired the name 'Windy'. In April 1920, his Sergeant Major evidently came into the barrack room and said: 'Gunner Breeze, you are drafted to Hood' and thereafter, he has always been known as 'Windy'. He recalled several interesting events including the lowering of the Union Jack when they went under the Forth Bridge on their way to Devonport for the first time when the sea - for once - was as calm as a pond. By way of contrast, he described the occasion off Vigo in heavy seas when they went to the rescue of the Admiralty Yacht 'Surprise' with Lord Birkenhead, the First Sea Lord on board and had to 'pour oil on troubled waters' on the raging seas, literally, until 'Surprise' was safely in calmer waters The fifth Newsletter, referring to the second year of the Association, opened with Fred's heart-felt expression of a sailor's sense of gratitude: 'Thank God for us being all Seamen of the seven seas - there is no greater Freemasonry than this.' He then said: 'From the county of Dorset, the home of the Admirals Hood, I wish you all the world over a Happy New Year' and his message ended with the following inspiring verse of Thomas Traherne's:

You will never enjoy the world aright
'till the sea itself floweth in your veins,
'till you are clothed with the heavens
And crowned with the stars.

Fred White's appeal for reminiscences in 1978 continued to bear fruit with several varied accounts of life aboard 'Mighty Hood'.

A. Thomas from Glamorgan, S. Wales who was 'fender boy' of the 2nd picket boat and later, the 'bowman', described an unusual 'cargo' carried on the 1926 Spring Cruise. With a Rolls Royce, a racehorse, a donkey, a pair of flamingoes and even a kangaroo that later went to a Zoo, it was a veritable menagerie. When Lady Hood heard about the mini-Zoo, she sent a more realistic 'mascot' in the form of a Bulldog pup! On another occasion, among all sorts of 'hardware' being hoisted aboard at Plymouth, Mr. Thomas remembered a combination motorbike and sidecar belonging to a commissioned gunner named 'Clickity Click'. When the then Commander, Arthur John Power, saw the 'combination' he ordered it off the ship and it was driven into dockside water by a contrite 'Clickity Click', to be salvaged years later. The writer became the proud owner of a more suitable souvenir - a glass-fronted case - which had been presented to the Chief Petty Officers' Mess during the World Cruise visit to Canada. Having hung on the Mess bulk-head, it became the subject of an ownership dispute when the ship paid off, happily settled by being given to him as the youngest, married man in the Mess.

Harry Smith from Portland, described an unusual experience during the 1926 Autumn Cruise known as the 'Gunnery Cruise'. During a North Sea trial when Harry was a Communications Rating, he was up on the Flag Deck with their distinguished passenger Admiral Earl Jellicoe when the ship's distress siren jammed open. As they were travelling at about 32 knots, the effect was so dramatic, it 'filled the whole North Sea with deafening noise and it took the Engineers ages to silence it'. To make matters worse, the bearings then ran hot and they lost speed to such an extent they only just had 'steerage way'. But somehow, just made it to Invergordon.

L. Hudson from Polesworth, Nr. Tamworth, wrote that he joined Hood in time to do the ten month 'showing the flag round the world' tour and left her in 1929. After the 1926 General Strike, they went to Portsmouth where he met his wife who came on board as a visitor. They married in 1930 but sadly, she died of cancer in 1974 and the poor man, then on his own at 77, wrote: 'I still have wonderful memories of my late wife and my other love, HMS Hood.'

The sixth Newsletter was devoted almost entirely to an 8-page account of Hood's spectacular life ending with the moving words of a German Naval Song:

'There are no roses on a sailor's grave,
No lilies on an ocean wave.
The only tributes are the sea-gull sweeps
And the tear-drops that a sweetheart weeps.'

By this time, in 1979, Association membership had increased throughout the U.K. and abroad. With a higher proportion of U.K. members living within easier reach of Portsmouth than Weymouth, it was decided to hold a Referendum to determine the most appropriate area for their functional H.Q. As the result was a majority vote in favour of a Hampshire base, a re-structuring of the Committee was effected and has remained almost unaltered to the present day.

To indicate his continuing goodwill, if not full approval of the move away from Weymouth, Fred White arranged to have a fine oak seat made, complete with a Hood plaque. Placed originally in the HMS Victory arena, it is now housed in the Royal Naval Museum, Portsmouth.

The lovely 900 year-old Norman Church of St. John the Baptist at Boldre in the new Forest, has always been the venue for the Annual memorial Service because of its special connections.

Among those who died with Hood in 1941 was Vice-Admiral L.E. Holland who had been a regular worshipper at the Church for many years, with his wife and family. The inner porch doors were given by them in memory of their son who died in 1936. Then, after the War when it became clear that no official memorial was likely to be raised for those who perished with Hood, Mrs Phyllis Holland instrumented a scheme which brought the Annual Service of Commemoration to Boldre.

The Church of St. John the Baptist, Boldre, Hampshire.
Venue for the annual Hood Association, Memorial Service.

Thanks to her inspiration, the porch holds a framed photograph of Hood, two Vice-Admiral's lanterns; a small stained glass window of St. Nicholas, the patron saint of sailors, and two long oak benches carved with the ship's badge of a Cornish Chough. The badge also appears in the set of kneelers at the altar rails in the North Chapel and on the runner in the front pew of the north western part of the Nave.

The area directly opposite in the north west corner of the North Chapel now features a very special Memorial - the Illuminated Book of Remembrance. This beautiful book, containing the names of all 1,418 sailors who perished with Hood, was written and illuminated by Mrs Daisy Alcock who was also responsible for the Royal Air Force Book of Remembrance in Westminster Abbey. Because the Hood memorial book is so special and needs very careful handling, there is also a facsimile copy for reference in the drawer beneath.

Thanks to a generous legacy, the benefactor's widow Mrs Cutlack, donated another book in 1997. This one - with names listed alphabetically, rather than by rank, for ease of reference-also has a cloth-bound copy for everyday use. Together they form a tangible memorial and are greatly valued by the Hood Association.

In addition to the written Memorial, there is also a wonderful picture of Hood painted and given most generously by the marine artist Montagu Dawson, in memory of his wife. The artist depicted the ship as seen from the quarterdeck of a destroyer on the starboard wing of her close screen. It bears the inscription: 'To the Glory of God, in honour of the officers and men of this great ship and in memory of Doris Mary Montagu Dawson 1899-1973'. Sadly that fine artist died a week before the dedication.

Near the Dawson picture is a Tampion that was used for preventing seawater from entering the 15in. gun barrels. It is believed that it came from one of the guns manned by the Royal Marines and was presented by Lady Binney, widow of a former Captain of Hood.

In every way then, except perhaps, in terms of space, the Boldre Church provides an ideal setting for the numerous relatives and friends who assemble each year to honour those who lost their lives with Hood.

Transfer to the Hampshire 'Base'

The Association's first AGM at their new, and continuing, Hampshire 'Base', was held on 25 May, 1980 at the Royal Sailors' Home Club, Portsmouth, following their Reunion Dinner the preceding evening.

The guest of honour was Vice-Admiral Eric Langley Cook who gave a most positive and memorable speech, a copy of which was promulgated for the benefit of those unable to attend.

He opened with unqualified praise for their hospitality and said: 'It was for me - a first timer-a fabulous experience. So superbly organised we might have been at the Savoy Hotel except that the company present was much nicer!' Later, he expressed his admiration for and gratitude to Admiral Sir Louis Le Bailly, Ted Briggs, Ned Johns, Fred White and the other old shipmates who launched and got the Association underway and steaming. He then described some of his experiences during three years in Hood during her 5th Commission, from 1931 - 1933, including the influence of different Admirals. After what the ship's Company thought was a satisfactory exercise, he recalled that their enthusiasm was quenched when they received a Flag Signal that read: 'Manoeuvre badly executed'. On the other hand, when another, from the genial Admiral, 'Bubbles' James arrived he said: 'I am proud to have joined you.' He inspired them all with explanation of the Royal Navy's peace-time purpose - to train for war in order to keep the peace; to show the flag and in home waters, to show the British public what they were paying for the ship to be a good Ambassador abroad.

Finally, in thanking them for the pleasure that being their Guest of Honour had given him, the Admiral said: 'My outstanding memories of the 'Mighty Hood' are her beauty at sea and in harbour and the magnificent quality of the ship's Company. I am so lucky and so proud to have served in her.'

At that time, in 1980, Harry Purdue who later became Chairman, was the Hon. Secretary and clearly maintained the high standard of communication already established. It is good to know that Windy Breeze proposed a vote of thanks to the wives who played a big part in helping them all carry out their work. Following another proposal, by Commander A.F. Paterson, a list of current members was drawn up and circulated and a vote of thanks was also given to the Vice-President for the beautiful bookcase presented to St. Anne's Church, Boldre, on behalf of the Association for the safe keeping of the Book of Remembrance there.

During the time that Harry Purdue was Chairman, he clearly enjoyed writing the Association Newsletters which were entertaining and informative such as one dated October 1984 in which he described a special meeting with the Lord Mayor who expressed a wish to establish a link between the Hood and Portsmouth. Harry said he felt 'ten feet tall wearing a new blazer with its special badge and the Hood tie' and, of course, replied to the Mayor in the affirmative. As a result, to start the ball rolling, a contingent of ex-Hoods was invited to stand on the Guildhall steps for the Armistice Parade on 11th November.

In a later Newsletter of October 1986, Harry had further interesting reports and events to convey to Members. First, as a result of a Royal British Legion member seeing the Hood Association Standard at Boldre in May and various 'intercessions' from the

Southampton Legion Committee, it was agreed that the Standard should be given a special place at the Southampton Guildhall Festival of Remembrance on November 17th.

Hood Association, 10th Annual Reunion Dinner 1986.
Hood survivors Bob Tilburn (standing centre) and Ted Briggs (sitting far right)
with members of the crew of HMS Electra,
the destroyer that rescued them after Hood's sinking.

Secondly, it was agreed that attendance by Hood Association Committee Members for their own Remembrance Day Service should be transferred from the Portsmouth Guildhall to the Naval War Memorial at Southsea- a custom that is still maintained.

Thirdly, gratitude was expressed for 'the warm welcome and hospitality always accorded to all by the Reverend Julian Richards and his Parishioners at that lovely old Church at Boldre for our own Memorial Service'.

Fourthly, he gave a graphic account of a memorable week's visit to Scotland by seven members and their wives. They travelled by bus to Glasgow and then transferred to a mini-bus for a tour that included Oban, Aviemore and Pitlochry and finished at Edinburgh where they had a special welcome from Eddie Goggins at the RN and RM Club. In exchange for the wonderful hospitality given by the resident Committee, a Hood plaque was presented and during the last evening, all enjoyed a modern version of the famous 'S.O.D.S's Opera, and a rousing rendering of a first World War song by shipmate Tom Shearsmith.

*Members of the Hood Association, at the Remembrance Service
at the Royal Naval Memorial, Southsea 1987.*

Finally, when back at their own base, the enterprising Tom helped
to clarify for the Committee, some problems arising from the presentation of a beautiful carved wooden plaque in Hood's honour
presented by a Maltese couple. When the donors, Mr and Mrs
Cassar, needed some financial assistance for a proposed visit to
England, arrangements were made to raise the necessary funds.

Chairman Harry excelled himself in his Newsletter dated July 1989
which opened with a glowing account of a memorable Reunion.
He said that 178 people sat down to a good meal with 'free Tots
for the males while the ladies' glasses were more decorously topped
up with wine'. Their guest of honour was Charles Strudwick and
his good lady Gwen who, when presented with an inscribed ship's
bell by the president Bob Tilburn, said they and their family would
treasure it for ever.   In his speech of thanks, Charles recited a most
appropriate poem of which the last lines were:

> 'For I have in my life that courage you gave
> When once I rubbed shoulders with you'

A raffle followed, 'the like of which had never been seen before'
because the prizes were splendid and the profit considerable!

Although it seems unlikely that another ship will ever bear the name 'Hood', it is still in use by a number of shore-based training establishments who have adopted it such as the 'Training Ship Hood' for Sea Cadets at St. Austell, Cornwall, and the 'Cadet Corps Hood' in Coboconk, Canada.

As usual, that year, the Church Parade at St Anne's, Portsea was headed by the band of TS Tenacity, followed by the ceremonial guard of TS Hood and ably supported by a group of indomitable ex-Hoods. Photographs taken and a Video made by Ken (Nobby) Clark's sons Bryan and John provided proof of their mobility and as Harry wrote: 'The spring may have gone out of our step but with chins in and chests out, we did not disgrace the uniform we once wore'.

A great surprise awaited them at the Boldre Memorial Service in the form of a visiting Padré the Rev. John Richardson an ex-Hood (1934/35) who didn't take long to prove it because on entering the pulpit, he exclaimed,' No Tot, just a glass of water!' During his Sermon which 'made them smile and made them think', he recalled his memories of Admiral James and Commander Rory O'Conor and later commended his congregation of ex-Hoods for being so friendly, attentive and reverent. He is evidently the author of several books, 'Jack in the Spirit', 'Jack in the Pulpit' and 'Jack in the Navy' of which the last caused Harry several late nights that he said was 'Well worth it'.

He then outlined a request from old shipmates of HMS Electra concerning donations towards the Chatham Memorial Window fund in memory of those who lost their lives in Chatham-based ships. It is strange that Electra was responsible for picking up the only three survivors from Hood and after an eventful Wartime career, she was herself sunk in the Java Sea.

Finally, details were given of a trip being planned by the Vice Chairman J.R. Williams, to TS Hood in St Austell.

The Reunion in June 1990 was a very special one for Harry because the preceding day he had married the charming widow of old ship-mate Tom Shearsmith.

Their Guest of honour at the Reunion was old shipmate Dixie Dean who recited an original poem about 'our Hood' and was presented with a ship's bell by the President Bob Tilburn. The presentation of a 5 and a half feet model of Hood by the clever maker R. Fletcher was another highlight, the only problem being where to house it safely and effectively.

On the following Sunday morning, the Church Parade was 'everything they would expect on Whale Island with flags flying and the band playing from the main dockyard gate to St Anne's Church' and attendance at the Boldre Memorial Service the next week was, as usual, 'bursting' at the seams to such an extent that extra chairs had to be found.

Finally, plans were discussed for the forthcoming year's very special 50th anniversary of Hood's destruction.

Tragically, Harry's happiness was very short-lived as he was killed in a car crash so John Russell Williams, always known affectionately as 'J.R.' took over as Chairman and wrote his first Newsletter in June 1990. He told members that an Audio Tape of the last Boldre Service was available and also a Video which included the lads from TS Hood, St Austell.

Their next big event was to be the laying up of their old Standard at TS Hood in September and would include an evening Reception with accommodation at a nearby Caravan Holiday Park. He ended with the cheerful exhortation, 'A Tot a day keeps the Doctor at bay'!

By August 1994, J.R. had become an experienced writer and was well into his stride with a varied and interesting Newsletter.

Parading their Standard at most of the commemorative D-Day events kept them all busy and prompted him to say, 'Hood is still well-remembered in these parts and I hope this is so everywhere else'. Such a sentiment epitomised the main focus of the Hood Association - to honour a great ship and those who perished with her.

The fact that a number of members were, regrettably, suffering from some of the infirmities of ageing, also had an honourable mention, his good wishes and reference to a notable exception, Mrs Annie Hurst who had just reached 102. She was the famous Hood widow (wife of Surgeon Commander Henry Hurst who went down with Hood) after a remarkable career of her own. She was known as the famous Hampshire War heroine - who for her work as a volunteer ambulance driver for the First Aid Nursing Yeomanry during World War 1 - was awarded the Croix de Guerre (the French equivalent of the Military Cross).

Hood Association founder members Harry Purdue and George Donnelly at the Memorial Service at Boldre 1987.

J.R. also recorded that shipmate Warrand (now of NSW, whose father, Navigating Officer Warrand went down with Hood) had made a generous donation towards a shield for the best Cadet of the year at both TS Hood, St Austell and TS Hood, Coboconk, Ontario. This inspired Albert E. Burton, the Association's gifted 'Knot man' to exercise his skills.

Next, he reminded members of Padré Ron Paterson's energetic programme of Cathedral Walks in aid of the Paterson Centre at Swanmore, his Parish for many years before his retirement. The Centre was established as a Memorial to Ron's late wives, Joan and Robin and his son Andrew who also, died most tragically, in his twenties. Ron, still remarkably active, if in his eighties, continues to work tirelessly for several other Naval Associations, in addition to being 'on call' to take local Services whenever required. One memorable walk to Guildford, for one of Ron's 'protégés', evidently started at Swanmore with Ted Briggs, J.R. and Den Finden with the Standard for inspiration. But they only proceeded as far as the old Vicarage where they were given a restorative glass of sherry! Then Ron and his fellow walkers went on their way to Guildford Cathedral.

By way of contrast, there was touching news from the children of Durness Primary School, Scotland who had re-painted the Hood stones on the Loch Eriboll hillside so they could be seen clearly from the road. (Durness School has now become such an established and much-appreciated part of the Association, they are featured in Chapter 6.)

Finally, J.R. reminded Members of all the Association functions arranged for the following year and expressed he and his colleague's thanks to Mrs Gladys Clark (wife of Treasurer Nobby Clark) for her hospitality and the provision of refreshments at their home, for all their Committee Meetings.

In his Newsletter of December 1994, J.R. outlined some of the Naval gatherings they had attended during the Autumn such as Trafalgar Day Service at Waterlooville, the Mountbatten Memorial Service at Romsey Abbey and the Armistice Service at Southsea where it was bitterly cold and windy as usual.

He then expressed Association thanks to Miss Warrand and also Mrs Jeffs (whose brother was lost with Hood) for their donations and to the redoubtable 'Knot man' Albert Burton and his 'Winger', Fred Carrington for completing the two shields. Arrangements were in hand for Albert and Commander Brown to present one to T.S. Hood at St. Austell and for shipmate George Donnelly of Toronto to present the other to Cadet Corps Hood in Coboconk.

They were all sorry to learn of Bob Tilburn's recent heart attack, Parade Master Roy Dumbleton's brain hemorrhage and also the illness of Sandy Powell in Dorset.

To cheer everyone up, J.R. was pleased to offer their thanks to Treasurer Nobby Clark for his excellent and continuing work in maintaining a 'healthy' balance sheet for the Association.

The A.G.M. in May 1995 represented a significant landmark in the life of the Hood Association for various reasons. First, it was announced that Bob Tilburn had sadly 'crossed the bar' but as the only remaining living survivor of 'our great ship', Ted Briggs was elected automatically as President - a position he has held ever since.

Following their success with a video of M.V. Derbyshire, Rob White, with David Mearns from the U.S.A. attended the Reunion Dinner and Boldre Service. Later, Ted Briggs conveyed to Members the outcome of a special Meeting with the two gentlemen. Plans had been discussed at length for supporting an expedition to locate and film the wreck of Hood and to conduct it with the utmost sensitivity and respect for the site as a 'War Grave'.

It was felt by all Members that the expedition would be a most appropriate way to commemorate the life and service of the Hood and all who sailed in her, particularly those who tragically lost their lives in her final battle. The proprosed T.V. documentary of the event would certainly provide a fitting memorial.

They also felt that 'detailed, recorded investigation of the damaged hull might answer the critical historical and technical questions about the cause of the explosion responsible for Hood's sinking. Finally, placing a Memorial Plaque on the wreck would provide some comfort for the many relatives of the casualties and would be much appreciated by all who had suffered from her loss.

Although it was stipulated that nothing would be touched if and when the wreck was located, the proposed project generated a considerable amount of controversy that led ultimately to correspondence with the Ministry of Defence.

It was finally agreed that as long as the expedition in no way contravened U.K. law relating to wrecks regarded as War Graves lying within U.K. territorial waters, as stated in the Protection of Military Remains Act 1986, it would be permissible. A note of warning was sounded however, concerning the absence of any enforceable International law protecting War Graves or other wrecks lying outside state limits.

The last part of the agenda concluded the Meeting, as usual, with more immediate matters such as details of local forthcoming events and encouraging news of increasing membership - then about 200 - but with an exhortation from the Treasurer for outstanding subscriptions to be paid as soon as possible.

J.R. then thanked Miss Warrand (daughter of Hood's late Navigating Officer, Commander Warrand) for agreeing to become Vice-President and Standard Bearer Den Finden for his sterling work on so many occasions.

Finally, with the wry humour, typical of so many ex-sailors, J.R. said he planned to give everyone a share of the big increase in his weekly Pension, 'a terrific 25 pence'!

The Summer Newsletter of 1995 described the Annual Parade for the Service at St. Georges, Portsea in which all, including 'poor little Cadets from TS Tenacity and TS Hornet were soaked to the skin and had to dry out in Church, and a wonderful Memorial Service at Boldre with beautiful singing and a rousing rendition of 'The Last Post' by Mr. Flood.

There was worrying news of a 'spot of bother with the crumbling west wall of St John the Baptist Church' that would evidently cost about £ 50,000 to repair, towards which a small donation from the Association was a welcome gesture of their appreciation and concern.

Earlier in the year, all were sorry to hear that the indomitable Annie (Nan) Hurst had died at the great age of 104 and had a Funeral worthy of a 'War Heroine' at a Church in Southwick where she had lived for 17 years. According to her nephew Henry, it was a very moving occasion and greatly enhanced by the presence of Association representatives including the Standard Bearer and 'a superb playing of the Last Post'.

At their Reunion, a model of Hood, made and bequeathed by the late Nobby Mould and presented by his widow, was auctioned to proud new owner Peter Heys. Members were all very sad to learn of 'Knot man' Albert Burton's death but pleased to hear how much his shield was valued by the Cadet Corps Hood at Coboconk who wrote: "Mr Burton's handiwork is unparalleled. It will be our Corps' premier trophy and we are very honoured to have it". They were also glad to learn that Vice-Chairman Tom Hooper was recovering from a stroke and pleased to celebrate Nobby Clark's 80th birthday with a magnificent cake.

Fred Carrington had made a nice shield for the Church at Loch Eriboll which it was hoped that someone holidaying in the far north, might deliver and J.R. expressed the committee's thanks to Dick Turner for keeping Minutes and confirmed that the annual subscription was still - at that time - a modest £3.50.

The Chairman's 1997 Newsletter contained a wide range of encouraging reports that emphasised the value of the Association as a lively channel of communication, especially as it was the first one ever to announce the setting up of a Hood Website on the Internet by an American enthusiast Frank Allen.

The Chairman's Autumn Newsletter of 1998 opened with an account of a memorable railway tour of Wales by a group of members in a train pulled by the engine 'Hood'. Arranged most efficiently by Vice-Chairman Peter Heys and his wife Jean, the new Association Secretary, the tour was like a Royal one as there were train spotters with cameras at every stop!

There was a slight variation in their usual November programme whereby the Standard was displayed at the Royal Naval Memorial on the 11th instead of the 17th at the Guildhall Square. President Ted Briggs laid a wreath in honour of lost shipmates and Den Finden dipped the Standard as the wreath was laid.

It was good to hear that Radio 'Ham' Malcolm Butler had contacted a wide range of Hood 'callers' over the air waves while a letter from American Internet enthusiast Frank Allen indicated that the Hood Website 'would keep our name and flag flying throughout the world'.

Then, J.R. thanked all who had helped in various ways throughout the year, including Rob White of I.T.N. Finally, he ended with one of his quips - hopefully not from personal experience -: Don't lend people money, it gives them amnesia!

Late in November 1998, Ted Briggs circulated a special letter to members reporting his visit to the Anglo Danish Society for a social evening to commemorate Remembrance Day and view the I.T.N Video, 'Mighty Hood'. In company with Rob White, producer of the Documentary, and Dr. Eric Grove, Naval Historian, Ted said he was Royally treated.

He welcomed the opportunity of expressing the Association's thanks to the Royal Danish Navy, the Commanding Officer of HDMS Triton, Captain Svend Madsen, RDN and the ship's Company for their kindness and consideration during the trip to Hood's 'grave'. As a gesture of appreciation, Ted presented signed prints of Hood and the Prince of Wales to their hosts and after the Video showing, the Chairman of the Anglo-Danish Society, Holger Casten and his wife Gurli, said 'There was hardly a dry eye in the house'.

The Chairman's next Newsletter, dated June 1998, was expertly presented in several colours, utilising for the first time special paper headed with the Association Hood crest. J.R. mentioned how nice it was to see so many people at Boldre including some new members and a warm welcome was given to Mike Collins from Australia who later laid the wreath at St. George's Church. Everyone was also pleased to see the Hon. Vice-Chairman Tom Hooper in the care of Jack Moulden who had kindly brought him from his Nursing Home. A group of Cadets from TS London arrived unexpectedly but looked very smart and were, of course, made welcome and - as ever - the bugler Alan Flood 'played perfectly'.

The Reunion was also very well-attended by 32 members including the 'star' Bill Stone, in his 99th year but still able to 'take a turn round the dance floor with young ladies'. The proposal that he should be Guest of Honour the following year was carried unanimously.

Links that have been forged between British and German Naval Associations indicate the level of understanding and fellow feeling that now exist between former enemies. In this connection, J.R's account of social activities following the A.G.M. is of particular interest because they were all entertained most enjoyably by a visiting Choir of German sailors led by Commander Grenfell.

President Ted Briggs was also presented with a German book 'Battleship Bismarck' by one of her last living survivors Josef Statz whose inscription is especially poignant:

With cordial greetings from one of the few survivors of
Bismarck to the sole living survivor of Hood in the
hope that such a stupidity never happens again.
From your German Navy comrade and survivor of Bismarck.

Josef Statz

There were also some more 'home-based' presentations: an engraved bell and ear-rings for Peter and Jean Heys in recognition of their much valued services and a plaque for J.R. himself from the Association to honour his sterling work over so many years.

Following a letter Ted Briggs had received from TS Hood concerning their recent acquisition of four new training rooms, Master Roy Dumbleton made a short, pertinent speech putting Ted's proposals for their naming, to the vote. It was agreed that the first three rooms should be called after the three survivors Briggs, Tilburn and Dundas and the fourth to be Warrand after the Commander who stepped aside to let Ted pass out of the Compass Platform in Hood - thereby saving Ted's life.

The morning after such an action-packed and convivial evening must have proved quite a challenge for some of the revellers. But one dedicated Committee stalwart, Treasurer Nobby Clark had to rise at 06.30 hours to talk on Radio Solent at 07.15 about his time in Hood.

All managed to muster later for the parade to St. George's Church under the command of Roy Dumbleton, 'still in good voice' and march to the rousing band of TS Tenacity with a Guard of Honour from TS Sultan. They were followed by the Association Standard and escort TS Tenacity's Standard, all the mobile members and the

German Choir. When they reached the Home Club, Ted Briggs took the Salute from the steps, thus setting the seal on a splendid ceremonial occasion.

As ever the St.George's Service was conducted in style by the Association Padré Ron Paterson who is always 'in good voice'.

In the last part of his Newsletter, J.R. thanked all concerned for the time and energy they continued to give the Association, including the Standard Bearer Den Finden and Dick Turner for his Master of Ceremonies duties. He also reminded everyone of diary dates to note for the coming Millennium year and, as always, wished everyone 'in sickness a speedy recovery' and 'God's blessings for all'.

Perhaps the only negative note was news of an increase in annual subscriptions to £5.00 and £10.00 for Overseas members. Considering the higher cost of postage and materials and the many benefits arising from membership, it seems unlikely there were any protests (although some members needed reminders of the rise later on).

J.R. ended with an appropriate thought: 'Worry is interest paid on trouble before it comes'.

The Millennium Year 2000 was an extra special one for the Hood Association because it coincided with their 25th Anniversary and Bill Stone's 100th birthday. During the annual Reunion, as their Guest of Honour, he was presented with a commemorative bell and responded with a spirited rendering of 'All the Nice Girls Love a Sailor' for which he received a great ovation.

After a celebration dinner, an auction was held of all the items generously given such as Fred Carrington's Knot Board and Jack Moulden's framed painting of Hood, the proceeds of which all helped to swell Association funds.

Their Sunday morning march to St. George's Church was well-supported as ever, with a 'wonderful turn-out by the smart lasses and lads of TS Tenacity and TS Sultan'. As their long-standing Standard bearer Den Finden was unwell and planning to retire, Tony Middleton kindly took his place and continues in that role.

Later, to mark Den's many years of Standard-bearing, the Committee gave him an inscribed pewter mug.

Mrs Bob Tilburn and J.R. took the salute at the March Past but just as they reached the Victory Gates at Portsmouth Dockyard, the heavens opened and everybody was soaked to the skin. It was quite a relief when they reached the dry, warm Church for the Service and the comforting ministrations of Padré Paterson. He undoubtedly established a precedent in the Order of Service when he broke off in the middle of his informal Sermon and asked Bill Stone to repeat his performance of the preceding night especially as the entire congregation - so inspired by his rousing solo, joined in with a rafter-raising chorus of 'All the Nice Girls Love a Sailor.'

During their march back to the Home Club after the Service, they were again soaked by a heavy downpour but were no doubt fortified by restorative Tots!

The Service at Boldre was equally memorable if or different reasons - they were packed out and it didn't rain at all. Later in the year, the indomitable Bill Stone laid the wreath during a visit from TS London and when John England came from Berlin to visit Portsmouth, he brought a Video tape of the German Choir's contribution to the 1999 Reunion.

It was good to hear of some unexpected contacts made with ex-Hoods while Commander Ken Evans was in Hospital and also that the Hood Website is going from strength, thanks to U.S. based Frank Allen, U.K. chief researcher Paul Bevand and an ever-increasing team of contributors all of whom help to maintain and extend Hood's influence throughout the world.

CHAPTER TWO

Mariners' Memories
A Focus On The Committee

President of The Hood Association,
Lieut. A. E. (Ted) Briggs M.B.E.
(From a CD Rom interview).

Ted's Early Days

Born in Redcar, Yorkshire in 1923, Ted developed an interest in the sea at an early age. His first glimpse of Hood was in 1935 when she came up the mouth of the River Tees. He badly wanted to go aboard but 'local fishermen charged' 5 bob a time to row visitors out' and his mother couldn't afford to pay for such a treat.

Even at a distance, Hood fired his desire to serve in her at the earliest opportunity. She had already established a reputation for being the most powerful warship afloat and the epitome of Britain's sea power, but Ted also recalls her remarkable 'grace' and says that he had 'never seen anything quite so powerful or so beautiful' even if, as he discovered later, her quarterdeck was virtually underwater when travelling at full speed.

He was 15 on 1st March 1938 and, without delay, joined the navy on the 8th. Initial training at HMS Ganges was harsh and restrictive, (the pay was only 5/3 per week for a Second Class Boy with one half-day off) if 'by and large a fair organisation'. Ted joined as a boy seaman but in the first fifteen weeks, decided he wanted to be a signalman and was lucky enough to be drafted to Hood in July 1939.

Life aboard was very different as 'all were treated as one of the company' and although they were partially segregated by being in a separate mess deck, they were treated well by the older sailors. He also claims that the relationship between men and officers was always good. Petty officers were in charge of all the boy sailors while 'the more senior officers seemed like 'God Almighty'.

With a total complement of 1,421, life aboard was very crowded and sleeping billets so inadequate, they had to sleep where they could, often in company with cockroaches.

Having joined Hood in 1939, Ted and his many companions were at sea when war was declared and they sailed at once to Scapa Flow to be ready for any surprise attack.

As Flagship, Second in Command to the Home Fleet, Hood was responsible for all the necessary signals and being a signalman, Ted's normal station was the Flag deck. He therefore had an excellent vantage point and his position proved to be his salvation later on.

At the start of World War Two the Royal Navy was entirely confident in their superiority and believed the German Fleet was quite inferior. It was known that Tirpitz and Bismarck were under construction but little was known of their size.

Action was expected almost at once as Hood's immediate job was covering convoys but their first experience was quite unexpected. When the enemy damaged the Submarine Spearfish in the Autumn of 1939, the C in C took the Home Fleet to sea in the hope of encouraging the German Fleet to come out.

According to Ted, 'they didn't but the German Air Force did! The Ark Royal was damaged and we had a near miss on Hood. I was on the Flag deck and saw aircraft approaching but didn't really register until the explosion occurred.'

They continued to escort vital convoys back and forth across the Atlantic and often felt very frustrated when they heard of ships being sunk by submarines when 9 times out of 10 they were just patrolling.

The next major incident that sticks out clearly in Ted's mind was the unfortunate sinking of the French Fleet at Oran in July 1940, following their collapse the previous month. He recalls that as flagship to Force H, Hood was ordered to carry out that unwelcome task, with Ark Royal, Resolution, Valiant, Enterprise and 11 destroyers. He describes it as 'absolute slaughter as they didn't stand a chance,' but, it was regrettably necessary to prevent French ships from falling into enemy hands.

Annihilation of The Mighty Hood

At that time they were The Flagship of Vice-Admiral Somerville but when they returned to Scapa Flow in October 1940, Admiral Sir William Whitworth succeeded him.

The German battle cruisers Scharnhorst and Gneisenau were known to be out in the Atlantic but escaped into Brest.

The next most significant report they heard in mid May 1941 was that Bismarck (the newly launched pride of the German Navy) had appeared and would attempt a break out into the Atlantic. The C in C decided that the area between Greenland and Iceland, known as the Denmark Strait should be covered. Meanwhile, the RAF had sighted Bismarck in Bergen. Hood had sailed from Scapa Flow but poor visibility prevented aircraft from surveying, apart from one flying boat.

Hood was about to enter the Denmark Strait when the County Class Cruisers Norfolk and Suffolk spotted both Bismarck and another heavy cruiser.

It was anticipated that the British ships should engage the Germans at about 2am on 24th May so Suffolk and Norfolk were detailed to report enemy movement. Unfortunately, Bismarck managed to chase them off successfully, and according to Ted 'we quickly lost radio contact and Admiral Holland in Hood, made the mistake of thinking Bismarck had turned back.'

By the time Norfolk and Suffolk had regained contact, Hood and Prince of Wales had lost valuable ground. 'Action stations' were sounded at midnight but heavy seas had resulted in loss of contact with the cruisers. So, by the time action took place, they were about 50 miles away. Bismarck was still only approximately 30 miles away but as Ted points out 'Hood's maximum gun range was, effectively, only 12 miles and her deck armour was thought by some to be thin and vulnerable.' Admiral Holland decided on a parallel course and at about 5am Bismarck was sighted from Hood's spotting tops. Due to radio silence, the 'pride of the German Navy' was taken by surprise and was therefore a target for Hood's guns.

Hood's third salvo evidently hit her adversary and caused significant damage that led to Bismarck's re-detection later on.

When Bismarck retaliated, no one could have possibly foreseen the catastrophic outcome of such a short engagement. When a 5th salvo from her powerful guns scored a hit at the base of Hood's mainmast, it penetrated the most vulnerable area just above the magazine and possibly, the controversial torpedo tubes.

There are numerous theories about the cause and nature of the disaster and many accounts of the stricken ship's last few moments afloat. But as Ordinary Signalman Ted Briggs was with Admiral Holland on the Compass Platform in company with the Captain, Navigating Officer and Midshipman Dundas, he was well able to observe all the immediate events.

Although at times still overwhelmed by the effects of his traumatic experiences, he can recall his memories with remarkable clarity. He remembers a sound, like the roar of an express train, and then the Gunnery Officer reporting a hit to the Captain.

Ted says that in the face of such as crisis, 'Reactions seem to occur almost automatically and a strange sense of unreality took over.' A calm running commentary was even maintained by the Padré for those on the lower deck until it was obliterated by the screams of those trapped and wounded.

Then things happened with such bewildering rapidity, it was impossible to record them except as a nightmare blur of sensation.

In fact, the whole terminal action lasted only five minutes and within three minutes of being struck, Hood went down.

The strange thing is that, as Naval witnesses in the area also observed, no explosion was heard. There was just an all-enveloping column of flame as Hood appeared to break apart and start to sink.

Fortunately for Ted, the Navigating Officer Commander Warrand kindly stood aside to allow him out, just in time. For the next moment he was aware of being dragged down, accompanied by a strange feeling of peace. Then he was aware of being shot to the surface and, as he gasped for breath, he saw the last of Hood's bows disappear beneath the icy waves.

The sea was thick with oil but remnants of fire illuminating the surface enabled him to see miraculously, a few Carley floats still drifting about. Even more miraculously, Midshipman Dundas, also on the Compass Platform, and Able Seaman Tilburn who had been on the boat deck were also still alive. Somehow or other, the three survivors managed to scramble onto a float and just glimpsed the Prince of Wales disappearing from view while she was still firing.

In spite of Hood's total destruction and the extremely unfavourable conditions, the C in C ordered a search just in case a miracle had occurred and any had escaped. Meanwhile, the three survivors clung to their raft in those freezing waters, struggling to withstand the numbing effects of hypothermia.

Suddenly, the sound of a flying boat broke through their somnolence and then Ted says: 'Dundas called out that he had spotted the destroyer Electra. I remember being pulled out by rope and having our frozen clothing cut off. We were then taken to sickbay where we thawed out, agonisingly.

Next, they were taken to the Mess deck and plied with Rum that, fortunately, made them sick, as they had swallowed so much oil.

After this initial 'First Aid' they were transported to Reykjavik where telegrams were sent to their relatives. When they returned to the U.K., they were evidently treated like Royalty but were not allowed to speak to anyone. On arrival at Greenock, they were met and escorted to London by an officer for a top security interview at the Admiralty with the Second Sea Lord.

It so happened that the Second Sea Lord was Vice-Admiral Whitworth who recognised Ted as the enthusiastic young sailor who had once - accidentally - collided with him and sent the Admiral flying!

After all the gruelling de-briefing, they were allowed to go on leave for 14 days 'in rough and ready uniform', pending a Court of Enquiry.

At the second Court of Enquiry, it was evidently agreed that their remarkable survival was probably due to a boiler bursting as Hood sank, so releasing an air bubble in which they were carried to the surface.

It was also agreed that none of those on the upper deck could have survived as they were either blown to pieces or sucked down with the ship while those below must have been suffocated and drowned. Ted says that 'They would not have had any hope nor would they have known much about it.' Perhaps the one consoling thought in this tragic catalogue of carnage is that few of the doomed company could have suffered for long.

In June, after their survivors' leave ended, Ted was assigned to HMS Mercury, ostensibly for a further period of recuperation, but it was interrupted by a second traumatic enquiry into Hood's loss.

After some varied experience in HMS Hilary, a Combined Operations H.Q. Ship and a short period at HMS Mercury as a Fleetwork Instructor, Ted was promoted to Leading Signalman in March 1942 and then, to Yeoman of Signals in 1943.

After the War, he remained in the Navy with a succession of appointments that extended his range and sphere of activity. He was promoted to Lieutenant in 1961 and awarded the MBE in 1973 for his loyal and sustained service. Following his departure from the Navy, Ted started a new career as a Furnished Letting Manager which continued until 1988.

When he joined the Hood Association, he had the distinction of being its youngest Member. Now, as the Association's much-respected President and sole living survivor of the 'Mighty Hood', he continues to lead a varied and active life, is much in demand as a guest speaker and has been frequently interviewed for Radio Programmes and Television Documentaries.

Robert (Bob) Ernest Tilburn

Who shared the Presidency with Ted Briggs for the first fifteen years of the Hood Association.

Bob Tilburn was born in Leeds on 3rd September 1921, the son of a police officer. His ambition to join the Navy sprang from a Navy Day visit to Portsmouth with his family when he was only ten years old.

A few years later when he was able to join, he underwent initial training and was then drafted to the Iron Duke (Jellicoe's Flagship at Jutland), then serving her final years as a Boys' Training Ship. After a few months in her, Bob joined Hood at Gibraltar in 1938.

During his first few months in her, Bob worked in the shell room which served 'A' turret but later, moved above deck to work on the 4' anti-aircraft guns. That job above decks, fostered his love of the sea and sea birds that were Hood's constant companions.

At the time of Hood's fateful encounter with Bismarck on 24th May 1941, Bob was at the 4' gun station on the port side of the ship. He recalled that although they expected some casualties, no one ever considered the possibility that The Mighty Hood could be sunk. Following a series of salvoes from her adversary, he was sheltering with two others of the gun crew when they were struck again - for the last time.

Bob's two mates were killed outright but he was evidently saved by the gun shield. Feeling very ill, he went over to the side and, to his horror, saw the ship's bows rearing up. Realising that Hood was going under, he had the sense to start stripping off surplus clothing that would jeopardize keeping afloat. But suddenly found himself in the water and was struck on the back of a leg by Hood's mast as she went down. Worse was to follow because an aerial caught one of his sea-boots and he was also pulled down into the icy waters. Remarkably, he was able to cut off the tangled boot with his knife and shot back to the surface. Once freed, he could see a lot of debris and some 'biscuit' floats in a thick carpet of fuel oil he was wary of swimming into.

After some time in the water, he was getting tired so decided to swim for a float. Having recovered one, he paddled to where he could see two other survivors and found Bill Dundas and Ted Briggs. The presence of companions was, for each of them, a strong factor in their survival. As time passed, Bob felt himself slipping away and even, welcoming sleep which, he had been told, would lead to a peaceful death. However, like Ted Briggs, he was kept awake by the indomitable Bill Dundas who kept on singing popular songs and kept the others awake. It was also Bill who first spotted Electra heading to their rescue.

After his attendance at the Court of Enquiry on the sinking of Hood, he was drafted to Victory at Portsmouth where he remained until 1943. During the next nine years, he had a series of varied assignments, ranging from service in Queen Elizabeth to a period in Air Sea Rescue before leaving the Navy in August 1952.

Married, with three children, Bob worked for the M.O.D. in Eaglescliffe and later, Inland Revenue until his retirement. His hobbies were reading, mainly detective books, winemaking and gardening - 'as a necessity'. Although he enjoyed some holidays in the sun, Whitby on the North Coast remained a life-long favourite because it helped to sustain his love of the sea.

When Bob joined the Hood Association in the mid 1970s, he became its second President, a post he shared with Ted until he passed away in February 1995.

Bob is greatly missed and will always be fondly remembered by his shipmates.

William J. Dundas

The third survivor of Hood

Sadly, very little is known about this third, brave survivor of Hood although he played such an active part in keeping his companions alert on their life raft.

Due perhaps to post traumatic stress and his family's wish for anonymity, William never participated in any peacetime Naval reunions. The information following was collected by Dave Weldon and is based on extracts from a Daily Telegraph feature dated 3rd November 1965.

After testifying at the first Enquiry into Hood's loss, William's next assignment prevented him from attending the second. He is believed to have served in other ships such as Neptune, Queen Elizabeth and Kingston and rose to the rank of Lieutenant Commander before retiring from the Navy.

With his wife Sylvia and their three children, he eventually settled in Orchertyre Lodge near Stirling but was mortally injured in a car crash near Tyndrum, Argyll in November 1965. When the Hood Association was formed five years later, his family were contacted but as they declined to become involved in any way, their wishes have been respected.

It is hoped however, that this brief outline of his life and bravery will serve as an epitaph to a courageous man.

Officers of The Hood Association

Chairman: John Russell Williams

'J.R.' - as he is known - was born in Aldershot, Hampshire during 1916 and, in due course, attended the West End Boys School. His father whose photo on a camel is a prized family treasure, had served in the Royal Flying Corps under the famous Colonel T.E. Lawrence of Arabia. But J.R. aspired to a sea-going career and joined the Navy when he left school, as a Boy 2nd Class. His pay then was only one shilling a week (5p in today's equivalent) and when he completed his training, it was increased to a lordly one shilling and sixpence (7.5p).

Drafted to HMS Suffolk, J.R. spent two and a half years on the China Station and he recalls attending the Funeral of the Japanese Admiral Tojo. He was then promoted to Able Seaman as a step towards being a Leading Seaman. When they returned to the U.K., J.R. was drafted to HMS Sabre, a First World War Destroyer. He says that their duties 'included chasing round after the Aircraft Carrier Courageous in case she flipped any of the aircraft into the sea'!

J. R. Williams, Chairman of the Hood Association. Seen here second from left as a Boy Seaman at HMS St. Vincent, with his parents and sailor brother.

When he left Sabre, he trained at HMS Vernon as a 'torpedo man' and when qualified, joined the 1st Submarine Flotilla at Malta. Following a wide range of duties in much smaller ships, J.R's first impressions of 'The Mighty Hood' must have been somewhat overwhelming. But like most of us, his memories tend to be selective and, in his case, spiced with his wry sense of humour.

Following his draft to Hood in January 1939, the ship underwent a short refit at Greenock and the installation of 'degaussing gear'. Suitably prepared, they went out on North Sea patrol under the command of Captain H.T.C. Walker known as 'Hookey' because owing to the loss of a hand, he had a hook in its place. As J.R. recalls, you could always tell when he was on his way by the warning clink made by the hook as he climbed up or down a ladder.

Fortunately for J.R. as he didn't 'like the main guns of Hood at all', his Action Station was in 'B' Turret, dealing just with electrical functions. According to him, a tube fired each gun and in the event of a malfunction, he would have to come to the rescue with his 20 volt lamp which he connected between the tube and the 'earth'. He also had a stand-by generator to bring into action if the turret had to switch to local fire control.

J.R. must have passed muster in every respect during his eighteen months in Hood because he was promoted to Petty Officer just before leaving her in July 1940.

The rest of his wartime years in the Navy were action-packed and ranged from control of Ratings drafted to foreign stations in ocean-going liners to training as a Torpedo Coxwain and several months with the dreaded Russian Convoys, including the famous PQ 18. J.R. describes that Convoy work as 'the worst days ever experienced' as they were bombed day and night from the time they left Iceland and 'life was so very short for many people'. At one point, they were iced in at Archangel for three months and on one of the return Convoys, the weather was so bad, individual ships had to make their own way back.

As J.R. was Coxwain of the Corvette Bluebell, he took the wheel while the ship was either at Action Stations or entering and leaving harbour. When she was the last ship to arrive back at Iceland, they were greeted with relief by those waiting. Unfortunately, their return was a mixed blessing for J.R. because continual bombardment had caused his ears to burst and he was sent first to Glasgow and then the Royal Naval Hospital at Haslar. Even after the end of the War when he was drafted to Concord for passage to the China Station again, his ears broke open once more and he was returned to the Barracks for further treatment.

J.R. spent the whole of his working life in uniform of one kind or another because when he left the Navy, he worked in Customs and Excise at Gatwick. There, by a strange coincidence, he got to know the brother of Admiral Jack Tovey who had been C in C of the Home Fleet when Hood was lost.

Now, finally retired, J.R. described himself as 'a geriatric' but he wears his Naval medals with pride for all ceremonial occasions, as do all ex-sailors. He has been Chairman of the Hood Association for many active years and is well-known for his pertinent and witty Newsletters.

Vice-Chairman: Peter Heys

Peter was born in February 1933 and educated at Rotherham Grammar School. Following his apprenticeship in electrical engineering, he studied at Imperial College, London where he graduated in 1958.

After nine years' work in the defence industry, he joined a major oil company as a Superintendent Electrical Engineer for their fleet of ocean-going tankers, then in 1982, became a pipe-line adviser to Europe and from 1990 until his retirement in 1995, worked for an Agency responsible for managing the Government pipe-line system.

During his career he travelled to many parts of the world and undertook assignments in Australia and Saudi Arabia, greatly widening his horizons and experience.

His interest in locomotives stems both from his engineering expertise and extensive rail travel in the U.K. He says that apart from the pleasure of railway journeys through the countryside, he always enjoyed the conversation with fellow commuters that often centred on the types and names of locomotives.

Shortly after returning to the U.K. in 1987 from his assignment in the Middle East, he was browsing through a bookshop and purchased a book on railway preservation. Stimulated by the book, he and his wife Jean became interested in the preservation movement and soon learned that the locomotive type hauling his commuter trains had something of a cult following amongst enthusiasts. This 'cult status' was probably due to their power, distinctive sound and the small number built, coupled with the fact they were all named individually after famous warships. This group of locomotives was categorised by British Railways as 'Class 50' for inventory purposes.

When the Hood locomotive was offered for sale in 1991, Peter decided to purchase it for preservation 'as it seemed the best and most reliable at the time'. He admits that it was a 'head over heart' decision but one he has never regretted because it became a line of communication with the Hood Association.

By one of those strange coincidences that often play such a significant part in our lives, Association member Dixie Dean was on a train to Boldre for the memorial Service in 1993 when he got into conversation with a railway enthusiast who was interested in the Hood emblem on this tie.

Vice-Chairman Peter Heys and his wife Jean Secretary to the Hood Association.

Knowing about the Hood locomotive, Dixie gave this gentleman his telephone number and as a result of this chance encounter, Peter learned about the existence of the Hood Association and contacted Ted Briggs who agreed to perform a re-dedication ceremony for the Hood engine at Alresford.

Following this memorable event, Peter joined the Association along with his wife, and has been an active and valuable addition to its ranks. In 1998, he became Vice-Chairman, to replace Tom Hooper who had to retire due to illness, and in 1999 was Guest of Honour at the Reunion Dinner.

Secretary: Jean Heys

Jean was born in February 1950 in Bournemouth. When she left school she trained as a secretary and was employed by a legal partnership until she became a full-time wife and mother.

Jean married Peter in 1985.

Fortunately, they share the same interest in railways and locomotives probably also due in Jean's case, to the amount of time she spent in rail travel throughout her life and her love of the countryside.

She became a member of the Association at the same time as Peter, in 1993 and has since given valuable support in every way. She agreed to becoming Secretary, in 1999 to fill a post that had been vacant for some time, and has proved her worth in every way. As a gesture of appreciation, she was invited also invited to the Reunion Dinner with Peter that year, when he was Guest of Honour.

Treasurer: Kenneth 'Nobby' Clark

Ken, more generally known as 'Nobby', was born in July 1916, in Street, Somerset. His father was in the Army but one of his brothers went into the Navy and his sister joined the W.A.A.Fs so all the Services were represented. He went to school for a while in Bristol but as part of a Service family, life was quite nomadic until they settled in Winchester in 1923. Apart from his time away in the Navy, Nobby has lived there ever since.

He left school at fourteen and had a series of jobs that included plumbing, lock-smithing and store-keeping with cycling at the weekends 'for fresh air and keep-fit'. He also did some weight lifting for increasing strength and muscle power.

When he was twenty, with war clouds gathering, a friend suggested he might join the Navy. At the Recruitment Office, he was disappointed to learn that he was too old to be a Physical Training Instructor but could sign on as a Stoker for twelve years. Having enrolled in this category and passed all the necessary mental and physical tests, he was drafted to Hood in September 1938.

Ken (Nobby) Clark,
Treasurer of the Hood Association.

The term 'Stoker' is perhaps, misleading because it conjures up images of stoking a furnace. This was applicable when ships were coal-fuelled but certainly not in Hood's day of oil-fired boilers.

Her size, weight and the speed required of such a powerful battle cruiser depended on an immense amount of fully functioning and expertly operated machinery. The geared turbines which could together produce 144,000 horse power, occupied three engine rooms while the 24 boilers were positioned in four boiler rooms.

In company with other Stokers, Nobby's place of work was in one of these boiler rooms and, as he points out in his recollections, the Stokers' main job was to provide an adequate supply of fresh water for the boilers and to fulfill all the basic requirements of the large crew. The supply came from seawater drawn and passed through condensers that converted it into fresh, distilled water. The Stokers were also responsible for testing the water's purity, using hydrometers.

Although the boilers ran on distilled water made by the condensers, they still became scaled up and had to be cleaned because it was dangerous for the tubes to become blocked as they could overheat or melt. It is no wonder then that so much emphasis was placed on Keep Fit activities because the Stokers had to crawl into various parts of the boilers to de-scale them with wire wool. As part of the cleaning process, one stoker would also be 'posted' to a large drum at the top with another to the bottom one. The man at the top would drop a ball bearing down each tube in turn while the man at the bottom had to ensure that it got through.

Not surprisingly, these challenging processes were carried out whenever possible, when the ship was in port.

Once oil tanks supplying the engines were empty, they also had to be cleaned by the stokers from inside and although clogs and rubber suits were supplied, they often leaked so the men preferred to work in the nude!

In addition, Stokers were responsible for ensuring that oil was drawn evenly from tanks throughout the ship. Dials were used for guidance to show whether or not the ship was on an even keel and if adjustments were required, oil was pumped from one tank to another, to restore the balance.

Maintenance of close contact between the bridge and engine rooms regarding changes in engine speed, number of sprayers required etc., was vital. The Chief Stoker was responsible for passing instructions to his team that he had received from above but methods of transmitting information were not as sophisticated as they are now. Nobby recalls: 'The normal manner for the Chief to communicate was by banging his spanner on a pipe; three clangs meant '3 sprayers needed ' So you had to be pretty alert to keep up and soon made yourself unpopular if you got the message wrong!'

Time away from their arduous duties both in their mess and above deck, was naturally therapeutic and memorable. Nobby recalls an incident concerning one of his mates who was a good cartoon artist. When Churchill visited Hood, the cartoonist Mickey Glenn did a sketch of their famous visitor and when the subject saw it during his tour of the ship, he thought it very good and autographed it. One of the Officers then announced that they would have it for the Wardroom whereupon, one of the Stokers said: 'No fear; the artist is a stoker' and 'it stayed with the lads'.

Like many of his mess-mates, Nobby was a keen Harmonica player in a special band known as the 'Hood Harmony Boys'. To supplement their concerts on board, they often provided entertainment in bars ashore for other sailors and locals and were rewarded with drinks.

He also remembers seeing the Cunard Liner Aquitania when she sailed into Gibraltar soon after he joined the ship and says: 'She was an impressive sight with her four big funnels.' While there, he palled up with some German sailors and was taken aboard their Pocket Battleship Deutschland. He was impressed by a large electric frying pan used for heating food on the mess tables and a glass boot 'Loving cup' that was passed round at meals.

Nobby left Hood on 2nd May 1940 and returned to Victory at Portsmouth. The following month he took an active part in the historic evacuation of Dunkirk and for nine days helped to ferry survivors to safety, using every kind of available craft, including rowing boats.

Apart from Hood, his next most memorable period of service was in the Minesweeper Boston from January 1942. Starting with a 'sweep' along the Lebanese coast, all along the North African coast and up to Malta and Sicily - which turned out to be the longest sweep in Naval history. Their varied experience included several near misses and support for the Sicily landings.

Since he left the Navy in 1949, Nobby has had a variety of jobs. He was a Bus Conductor for a while and then a Caretaker at Western Primary School. Finally, he worked at the Telephone Exchange for thirty years before his retirement. He and his wife Gladys who were married in 1946, have always had a happy and settled family life with three children, three grandchildren and now one great grandchild.

Nobby says he has no time for any hobby except the all-absorbing interest of the Hood. He joined the Association soon after its formation and has served as Treasurer for over twenty years.
He is renowned for his astute and meticulous handling of all matters financial and for the prodigious amount of time and energy he devotes to maintaining contact with Members far and wide.

As the focal point of communication of every kind, Nobby has amassed a wealth of material through the years and has become the Association's unofficial archivist. In fact, this book owes its inception to the use of the Archive collection for which the author is profoundly grateful.

Meeting Secretary: Dick Turner

Born at Wilton, near Salisbury in January 1918, Dick fulfilled his boyhood ambition when he entered the Navy in February 1936. His initial training consisted of 8 weeks 'square bashing' followed by 8 weeks mechanical training in all the types of machinery they were ever likely to encounter.

He and his fellow trainees joined Hood in September that year and he says that most of his 'mates' stayed together for the next three years and some for even longer.

As a junior Stoker, Dick's duties involved tending some of the machines in Hood's middle engine room to ensure they were all working correctly. Progression through a scale of grades was supervised and recorded by the Divisional Officer and Dick says, with characteristic modesty: 'I was fortunate enough to be graded 'Superior' throughout my period of service'.

According to Dick, Hood's dimensions and the size of her crew precluded extensive social mixing. As an alternative, he enjoyed shared activities with a small group of friends some of whom he can still remember by name such as: 'Taffy Thomas, Charlie Scrammel and 'Kab' Kelloway. He also had a school friend Howard Blake, in HMS Barham with whom he maintained contact for many years. Howard was a Signalman in the Navy but later joined the Fleet Air Arm and rose to the rank of Lieutenant Commander. Dick admits that he emulated his friend's example but when he expressed a wish to join him, was told that the Navy had spent too much time and money training him to consider his release.

Among his off-duty, Keep Fit activities, Dick recalls swinging Indian clubs on the Boat Deck, swimming races alongside and team competitions between Cutter crews.

Despite such welcome diversions, the Spanish Civil War dominated political events during most of Dick's time in Hood. The ship's presence provided a deterrent to General Franco's insurgents and security for Convoys of British merchant ships. One incident that still stands out centred on a merchant vessel whose intrepid Captain was known as 'Potato Jones'. Thanks to Hood's protection, he made a last minute 'run to Bilbao' just before the port fell to insurgent forces.

During Dick's next twelve months in Hood, he was an Auxilliary Watch Keeper, still in the middle engine room and other outside spaces as one of a team of four, responsible for whatever equipment had been allocated by the Engineering Officer of the Watch. He has a vivid memory of Louis Le Bailly, then Lieutenant in charge of the Watch, now Vice-Admiral Sir Louis Le Bailly, author of 'The Man Around the Engine'. This unusual and absorbing autobiography provides a graphic insight into 'Life below the water line' in peace and war, including his time in Hood from 1932-1933 and again, from 1937-1939.

Dick recalls that when Hood returned from England to the Mediterranean, Admiral Blake who had been in Hood during the Spanish Civil War, had a heart attack and was replaced by Admiral Andrew Browne Cunningham, 'A.B.C.' who was later considered by many as the foremost British Admiral of the War.

There was also a change of Captain a few months later when Captain Pridham was replaced by Captain 'Hookey' Walker - also remembered vividly by 'J.R'. Dick says that the hook in place of a hand was the subject of much speculation especially when it was claimed that 'he wore a gold one for Sunday Divisions'!

Dick Turner,
Meeting Secretary of the Hood Association.

The day they sailed for home happened to coincide with Dick's 21st birthday. He says that not only was going home the best present he could have had but 'the real bonus of reaching that age was not having to attend Gym sessions on the Upper Deck at 0700 every morning'. By the time Dick left Hood in November 1939, he had acquired a few nicknames such as 'Nutty', attributed to his taste for nut chocolate, as well as 'Tiddly' and 'Blue' (of undisclosed origin!)

During the next few challenging wartime years, Dick became a Leading Hand Petty Officer and served first in the Corvette

Gladiolus, then in Vetch and finally Whitshed, a veteran destroyer built in 1918. The contrast between his first great ship and Gladiolus was considerable. As Dick recalls: 'Even in the Mighty Hood, there were times when the swell was so great you would lose sight of other ships in the flotilla apart from their top masts. But the effect of heavy seas was even more pronounced in little Gladiolus'.

Fortunately for Dick, if tragically, for all those who lost their lives, both his first ships were sunk within six months of one another after he left them. Despite the hazards of intensive convoy work and several near misses, Vetch was more fortunate. She also earned some distinction for convoy protection under the command of Captain Walker who was awarded a DSO and several Bars for his unique and successful anti-submarine tactics. Dick recalls that another of Captain Walker's claims to fame was the origination of a custom to 'splice the mainbrace' every time a U-Boat was sunk.

He points out however, that the stress of continual convoy work on all the crew was extremely wearing and long lasting. There was little chance of any restful sleep because the Action Stations bell would sound at any time of the day or night. The effects of stress were brought home to him most forcibly when he was ashore with his wife at Liverpool for a short leave during the war. Awoken by their alarm clock in the morning, he leapt out of bed, grabbed his clothes and was heading for the door when his departure was halted by his wife, calling out 'Whatever are you doing, Dick? As Dick says: 'In my mind I was still in my ship and the Action Stations bell had sounded. My reaction was completely automatic and a sign of the high state of nervous tension in which we all lived in those days'.

Standard Bearer: Dennis Finden

Den served in Hood from May 1938 until May 1939 (Overlapping with Vice-Admiral Sir Louis Le Bailly, Nobby Clark and Dick Turner).

As a Boy Sailor, he spent a month or so on the Admiral's barge but when he 'lost two boathooks' which were considered expensive in those days, he was evidently 'demoted' and assigned as a Watchkeeper. In this role, he was one of four - two Seamen and

Dennis (Den) Finden
Hood Association Standard Bearer

two Marines - who shared the watches throughout each twenty four hour period. His other role, and clearly an enjoyable one for which he was well-suited and kept for three years - was as a bugler.

When he left the ship, he had attained the rank of Petty officer and, like so many others, he recalls his service in Hood at such as critical time, with affection and gratitude and maintained contact with some of his shipmates for many years.

Later in the War, he was captured at Tobruk and became a Prisoner of War. He managed to escape after only a few days and 'made it back to Suez with the help of a Carley Float and the assistance of Air Sea Rescue'.

As a founder member of the Association, like Nobby, Den has played an active part in the life of the Association for 26 years which included 14 years as Standard Bearer.

Padré of The Association
Reverend Ron Paterson

Reminiscences of a Boy Sailor in Hood 1933-1936

After a year's training at HMS Ganges, Ron was 'lucky enough to be drafted to Hood at the age of 15+ when a group went up to join her at Rosyth in November 1933.

He recalls: 'We went up by boat to join that beautiful ship as she was lying under the Forth Bridge and were welcomed by a very fine figure, Commander Rory O'Conor. I remember that his Standing Orders were unique. Known as the Ten Commandments, they established the right code of conduct for ourselves and the ship. They were quite ordinary in some ways, concerning discipline and good manners but they were easy to follow and appropriate to the needs of the crew for all occasions. He had such a prodigious memory, he learned the names of the entire ship's company - an extraordinary feat that gave me an example to follow later when I commanded my own ships.

Although there were various Divisional Officers in charge of us, he was concerned with overall organisation at every level and was renowned for his accessibility which he called 'The doctrine of the ever open door'. Later on, when I was responsible for a ship's company, I followed the same Policy and said ' I have an ever open door. If you wish to come and seem me about any matter of personal concern, you are welcome at any time, unless it is a matter of discipline when you will have to go through the usual channels.'

Returning to his life in Hood, Ron outlines his work and progress as a boy sailor and says: 'There was never a dull moment as most Ganges boys realized they would have to work hard at everything especially as there was so much competition on the lower decks in the thirties. My first stepping stone was working for the Higher Education Tests - a very hard job but I did achieve my objective, H.E.T.'s for Commissioned Rank and I also became a Seaman Gunner. Normally, young seamen went to Whale Island but as Commander O'Conor was a Gunnery Officer, he arranged a special course for us while we were there and we became known as the 'Jubilee Seamen Gunners'.

They were also encouraged to join in all the available Keep Fit activities afloat and ashore. At one time, when required to save fuel, Hood spent many weeks lying alongside the South Mole at Gibraltar. In order to ensure that no-one went astray, the Commander arranged for a large empty shed to be turned into a Cinema and Sports Complex for every kind of recreational sport

Towards the stars! A very young Ron Paterson in the muzzle of one of Hood's 15 inch guns. The Reverend Ron Paterson is today Padré to the Hood Association.

including Gymnastics and Boxing, at which Ron excelled. They also played Water Polo and took part in all the field sports it was possible to be involved in. Recalling some of their achievements, Ron says: 'Hood generally won everything - she was a very difficult ship to beat with such a truly wonderful atmosphere and a very high morale'.

Ron also has a vivid recollection of some special events during Hood's 1933-1936 Commission, such as the unfortunate collision between Renown in 1935: 'Being a curious sort of chap, I was on the Upper Deck during the exercises and happened to be on the Starboard Boat deck when I saw that huge ship coming towards us. Even I thought it was a bit close! Hood was obviously trying to turn away but Renown continued and struck us on the starboard quarter with such force that all the guard rails went for six and a bit was even knocked off the propellors. It was certainly quite an experience but it could have been worse.'

The Fleet Review at Spithead in honour of King George V's Jubilee in July 1935, was a much happier event of which Ron has some unusual memories: 'There was a colossal collection of ships of every type. I was in Hood and at night time when we were already illuminated, we were all given candles. At a signal, we had to light them and the effect, lasting for about ten minutes, was remarkable

- an almost unending line of flickering lights along the guardrails, right along the ship. Later, we were told that when His Majesty inspected us and we all shouted 'Three Cheers', we were to say 'Hip Hip Hooray', not Hoorah!'

The grand finale of the three years was the 1000th day of a memorable Commission. Ron says: 'It was a truly wonderful occasion when Rory was in his element and did everything possible to celebrate, including a performance of the Ships' Own Dramatic Society. It was indeed outstanding as most Commissions do not exceed two and a half years. Ron concluded his reminiscences of life in Hood with this appreciation: 'To sum up, any one with an ounce of commonsense and determination could achieve advancement in the Navy, with Rory O'Conor's help. Most of the boys became Petty Officers although, sadly, many didn't survive the War. Fortunately, I got away with it. Nobody could have done more than he did in preparing the Navy for War and his influence was felt by hundreds of young people. When we all heard about the sinking of Neptune in December 1941, we all realised that his death was a tragic loss to the Navy.'

When Rory O'Conor was promoted in 1936, Ron had already left Hood and went - ironically - to Neptune. He did achieve 'considerable advancement' as a Lieutenant Commander in successive command of four ships during and after the War, including two Minesweepers of the Algerine Class. On leaving the Navy in 1958, he was ordained and served as Vicar of Swanmore for 23 years. Now a widower, he lives in nearby Bishops Waltham, not far from some of his extensive family.

His Swanmore connections are still perpetuated through the Paterson Centre, initiated as a Memorial to both his late wives and son Andrew. Although in his mid eighties, Ron continues to enjoy and active life in many areas, ecclesiastic and secular, including regular Golf. He is frequently asked to take Services, often at short notice and continues to be Padré of several Naval organisations including the Hood Association.

CHAPTER THREE

'Mariners' Memories'
from Members of the Association
Through the Years 1920-1934

WINDY BREEZE
Hood service: 1920-1922

Early days aboard the 'Mighty Hood' by a Blue Marine

Windy is one of several Association Members who had vivid memories of Hood in her early days. Following a course at the Fort Cumberland and Gunnery School, Eastney, Gunner Breeze was sent to HMS Glorious for training on the single 15' gun turret, similar to Hood's class C Guns. When told by the Sergeant Major in April 1920 that he was drafted to Hood, he was instantly dubbed 'Windy' and retained the appellation thereafter (as already mentioned in an excerpt from Fred White's 4th Newsletter, Chapter One, p53).

'Windy's first sight of Hood was at Rosyth in the King George V dock - the only one large enough for her - where he said: 'She stood like a Queen and certainly we were very proud to have been chosen to serve in such a magnificent ship'. He says that on their way to Devonport for the first time 'the sea was as calm as a pond', unlike what they would experience later and then describes the goodwill trip to Scandinavia as the most interesting he had ever experienced, with many ceremonial guards of honour and Royal visitors.

After their Christmas leave, they had a spring cruise in 1921 to the Med. and a change of command to the forbidding Captain Mackworth. Windy recalls some memorable moments such as when the Captain, who often asked for a dozen marines when work was required, received a dozen tin soldiers through the post! All the actual Marines had a handwriting test and leave stopped for 14 days but the culprit was never identified.

There was another occasion when a visiting goat was pushed down a skylight onto the Admiral's bed, but history doesn't relate the consequences. Windy also recalled that when Hood was at Gibraltar with the US battleship 'Maryland', she was described as a 'mighty fine picket boat' by the Yanks.

On a more solemn note, when they returned from the Med. early in 1922, the entire fleet stopped off Land's End at approximately the spot where the submarine K5 went down, to hold a Memorial service. Wreaths were cast on the waves (as they were at Hood's Arctic grave nearly 60 years later); something Windy remembers every time he hears the hymn 'Eternal Father.'

Hood Sailors and Marines at rifle practice beneath the Rock of Gibraltar.

In May 1922 Windy was so affected by the Geddes Axe and its effect on promotion, he obtained his release from the Navy and returned to Eastney.

He completed his recollections by saying 'I enjoyed every minute of my stay on board with such a happy ship and I'm delighted there is a flourishing Hood Association which I am sure will live up to that famous ship'.

WILLIAM FREDERICK STONE

Mini-Biography of a Remarkable Centenarian
1921-1924

William, 'Bill', was born in S Devon on 23 Sept 1900, the 10th child of a family that eventually comprised 8 girls and 6 boys.

His father worked around the local farms and could do most jobs that cropped up such as operating agricultural machinery and slaughtering and butchering pigs. Bill and all his brothers helped their Dad when required and acquired some informal biology lessons.

As four of Bill's uncles had served full time in the Navy, it was almost a foregone conclusion that he and several of his brothers would maintain the family tradition. After leaving home, aged 13, he had to 'mark time' with a series of local jobs, including driving a steamroller until he was 18 and able to fulfil his ambition.

He signed on eventually at Plymouth at the end of the First World War but his initial training was interrupted when he and many other recruits were assailed by the 1918 outbreak of virulent flu. Having survived their tough treatment, including 'fumigation', he returned to good health and received his first draft, to join the Battle Cruiser HMS Tiger at Rosyth. A further delay was caused by the 1919 rail strike when he was sent to South Wales for 'essential work on the railway' as his papers revealed him as a 'driver'!

While he was in Tiger, Bill he had the opportunity of exercising his characteristic initiative when he 'started to look around for a spare time occupation' that would enable him to supplement his Naval pay and opted for tobacco rolling. But it was after leaving Tiger in 1921, while awaiting his next draft at Devonport, that an even more lucrative sideline materialised. It so happened that he met an old chief in barracks, retiring from his job as a Naval barber and wanting to sell his equipment. Thinking it might be a good way to earn some extra money in his next ship, Bill bought a full set of clippers, comb and scissors for just £1. Little did he realise then that this purchase marked the start of a career that would even outlast his days in the Navy.

A further surprise awaited him for when news of his draft to Hood came through, he was the only one joining on the day. He lost no time in putting his barbering skills to the test, once he was aboard, especially when he learned that the ship had a fitted barbers shop. Fortunately for him soon after his arrival, he was recommended as a replacement for an unsatisfactory hair cutter and he took over to share duties and takings with a Marine Bandsman.

Bill says: 'The Barber's Shop' in Hood, on the port side of the upper deck, was a lovely room with 6 foot wide mirror, water geyser and all the equipment a budding barber needed. He was even able to sling his hammock up in the corner where there was far more room than on the mess decks.

There was never any shortage of customers and apart from a showdown with his partner who was found to be purloining more than his share of their takings, it was a highly successful enterprise. Sometimes, he even accepted bottles of beer from officers in lieu of payment as a change from the daily issue of rum.

Bill also found that being a barber often enabled him to hear what was going on! When they were at Gibraltar during the Spring Cruise of 1923, he extended a commander's haircut time so that he could listen to a conversation with the Engine Room Commander. He gathered they were discussing the tricky question of clearance if Hood went through the Panama Canal - the first he heard of the famous Empire Cruise.

With his phenomenal memory, Bill can recall a number of unusual incidents during their eleven months away and he also retains an extensive range of anecdotes. He says first, that all in Hood were fascinated by the equipment they took with them, including a Rolls Royce, with driver. Required for ceremonial occasions, it must also have been an excellent way of showing off the best of British motor cars throughout the Empire.

Next Bill remembers to this day, the extreme heat in Sierra Leone. It was so intense that a seaman who went ashore with the film crew returned with severe sunstroke. Barber Bill was required to shave the man's head for a necessary application of ice packs and was not exactly popular when the patient recovered!

Continuing with the World Cruise itinerary, Bill was initiated into 'the line' ceremony when they were hailed by King Neptune and his court for the 'order of the bath', experienced the wild 'south-easter' storms around South Africa; were greeted by the natives of Zanzibar with great bunches of bananas and other tropical fruit and he bought in Singapore a £5 tea set which is still in use.

Once they reached Australia, they were overwhelmed by the welcome accorded them, especially during 'open days' when visitors were allowed free entry to almost any part of the ship. Bill remembers that 'some of the younger chaps were quick to pick out the best spoken and best dressed of their guests in the hope that good tips would be forthcoming at the end of their guided tour!' He also recalls the occasion when acting as a guide in the engine room, packed to capacity, he showed two ladies round and spent some time explaining the circulation and condensing system. Only later did he discover that their husbands were Engineer Officers so they probably knew it all but maybe they passed back a good report of that eager young stoker!

Apart from the beauty of Hobart, Tasmania, Bill remembers a 'small diplomatic incident' occasioned by the Admiral's unfortunate gaffe in a speech ashore. Apparently he said that 'The Navy today mainly consists of men drawn from prison whereas in earlier times they had come from good homes'! Of course, he had meant to say it the other way round but the papers were soon full of it and he had to make an apology. Any of the crew going ashore were also treated to good-humoured leg pulling centred on the amount of time they were 'serving'. Bill even remembers one of the many question and answer jokes, 'Why is the Empire Cruise like a Ford car?' and the answer 'Because the Hood is the best part of it!'

They arrived in Wellington, New Zealand, on 24 April 1924, just before ANZAC day and many were involved in a ceremonial march through the city. Hood's stay there had personal significance for Bill because he obtained seven days leave, at short notice, to stay with some relatives who had emigrated in 1920 and showed him all over the city.

Before leaving Wellington, Bill recalls they were honoured by a visit from Admiral Jellicoe, then Governor of New Zealand, who travelled with them to Auckland. Lucky Bill was allowed further leave for a trip to Rotorua led by Admiral Brand who was in command of the Light Cruiser Squadron. Bill still treasures some Maori 'titbits' such as these, 'We used to have wars but we let the British do that for us now' and 'When Captain Cook's pig fell into the hot springs, everything was rescued bar the grunt!'

Bill remembers their next stay in Honolulu for two things, the very modern docks and the fact that no drink was available due to Prohibition!

The squadron then continued its journey across the Pacific where a contingent of the crew, including Bill, were scheduled to travel by train through the Rockies and rejoin the ship at Halifax. Much to Bill's delight, his request for permission to stay on board was granted so that he could experience Hood's amazing passage through the Panama Canal, he describes as 'the highlight of the entire cruise'.

As the Commander had suspected (in a conversation overheard in the Barber's shop 12 months before), the clearance on either side of the canal's locks was minimal and Bill says: 'As the lock filled it was incredible to think that water alone could lift Hood's 40,000 tons with apparent ease'.

The last 'lap' of the World Cruise 'took in' Jamaica, Halifax, Quebec and Newfoundland before they crossed the North Atlantic en route for home. When they reached England, Bill had the grand total of £100 from his barbering - a great deal in 1924. But his request for an extended stay in Hood was rejected because the commander pointed out that as he had done seven years in the Home Fleet, he was due for Foreign Service. Bill says 'Not long afterwards, I found that even if I had managed to convince the Commander of my value to the ship, it would have made little difference as Hood was transferred from Devonport to Portsmouth and I would have left her anyway'.

Lest anyone should think that Bill's time in Hood was mainly confined to the Barber's shop, it should be stated that he was often on picket boat duty which involved solo responsibility for the small engine room and he says that 'By the time I left Hood, I think I had done every possible thing a stoker could do'.

The year 1941, as Bill recalls was one of the grimmest of the war. The devastating news of Hood's loss on 24th May affected him deeply, 'Those were the darkest days - the only ones in the war in which I really felt down'.

Centenarian Bill Stone stands proudly before the big Naval guns outside the Imperial War Museum, London.

When Bill left the Navy, he moved back to South Devon and after recovering his 'land legs' for a while at a barber's shop in Plymouth, he set up his own business in Paignton which he ran for

24 years. Following his eventual retirement at the age of 68, he and his wife Lily spent 16 happy years at Broadsands near the sea where they had a lovely house and beautiful garden in which he spent a lot of time. Later, they moved up to Watlington to be closer to their daughter and the rest of the family and made many new friends, several of whom were in the war or had experienced service life in peacetime. With his wife, he became a regular churchgoer and had the distinction of being confirmed at the age of 88.

When Lily died, after years of crippling arthritis, he received a great deal of support from friends and neighbours and at 100 years old, says:

'Many people are interested in what I have done and seen throughout an eventful life. I am a member of several Associations:-

> The 'Hood' Association;
> The 'Newfoundland' Association;
> The Dunkirk Veterans Association, High Wycombe Branch;
> The Dunkirk Veterans Association, Henley Branch;
> The Royal Naval Association, High Wycombe;
> The Western Front Association, Reading;
> The George Cross Island Association; and, of course
> The Royal British Legion.

I enjoy being the oldest member of all these Associations and the little privileges that age brings me. When the Association of Dunkirk Little Ships (veteran ships from Dunkirk) sail up the Thames to Henley each July, I have had the honour of joining Raymond Baxter, who is the Commodore of the Little Ships Association, aboard his boat L'Orange. In 1999 when we arrived at Henley I was announced as the oldest member and presented with a bottle of Champagne.

Locally, I am a member of St Leonard's Church where I have made many lovely friends. Jenny and Richard regularly take and fetch me as it is a little too far for me to walk.

Other local friends - Rupert and Renee; Don and Daphne; and Frank take me to my Association meetings and outings. My daughter Anne and her husband Michael take me to the Reunions of my old shipmates and, during the summer of 2000, took me back to Devon for a week - a trip down memory lane for me which I very much enjoyed.

My grandson, Christopher, is now 31 years old. He is not married yet, but after his studies spent three years travelling around the world by himself. I told him that the Navy paid me to do that! He is now a senior electronics engineer working in the UK.

My granddaughter, Susie, is 27. She also is unmarried and lives in Albany, New York State, USA working as a project co-ordinator for a Research Agency in Criminal Justice.

I feel sure that someone has been taking care of me over all these years. I only have to think back to the instance at Dunkirk when, with ships sinking all around me, I said 'God, help us' - and He did.

People often ask me what I attribute my long life to. I tell them that I put it down to three things: A Contented Mind; Clean Living; and Trust in God.'

RECENT UPDATES
Bill as Guest of Honour in 2000

During 2000, Bill was the Guest of Honour at both the Reunion of the Hood Association and the Newfoundland Association. At the Hood Reunion, he was presented with a brass ship's bell which now adorns the hall in his home and after the Reunion dinner, he made a speech and treated all present to a rendition of his favourite solo, All the Nice Girls Love a Sailor.

Bill on the Hood Website in 2001

In the year 2001, Bill has even become acquainted with the Hood Website! When he was shown the Empire Cruise Photo Album by friends at a reunion some time ago, he was naturally keen to have a copy of his own. By chance, an American book collector had found one in a charity shop but as he thought it should go to someone closely connected with Hood, he made contact with Frank Allen who runs the Website in the USA. Frank then put him in touch with Paul Bevand, the UK Internet researcher who in turn, contacted Bill's family. Eventually, after 77 years, Bill became the proud owner of this special commemorative album.

The second occasion concerns an old friend Harry Cutler who had also served in Hood during the Empire Cruise. When he saw Bill's name on the Hood Website, he contacted him and they had a good, long chat exchanging memories of the famous cruise all those years ago. They have since had further conversations and hope to meet again some time.

FRANK HIORNS
Nearly a Centenarian
Hood Service: 1922-1923

Frank was born in February 1900 and lived in Stoke Park, near Gosford Green, Coventry, only a few hundred yards from the City football ground. Attendance at a match when he was only seven years old engendered a life-long interest in the game and he developed such talent he could have made it his career. But he chose the Navy instead and joined the Service in 1915, signing on for twenty years. He was trained as an engineer and survived the remaining years of the First World War without major traumas or injury. He can remember the scuttling of the German Fleet at Scapa Flow in 1919 and acquiring a pair of binoculars from a German battleship, which he used for the rest of his life.

For his first most memorable draft, he joined the crew of HMS Argus, the first 'flush-deck' aircraft carrier. The second and most special appointment was to Hood in 1922 as a member of her first crew. When she sailed to Rio de Janeiro that September for the 100th anniversary of independence, the Brazilian Government requested the British Admiralty to send players to represent the Royal Navy at football, boxing and athletics. As Frank had already proved his prowess, he was nominated captain of the football team and after winning the match, had the honour of shaking hands with the Brazilian President. Back in England, Frank's proud family was able to see films of the matches, thanks to Pathè Gazette. He had already won a boxing trophy for a Naval featherweight championship in 1919 and later took an active part in athletics, cricket, golf and bowls. Frank also had the interesting experience of crossing the Line in Hood during 1922, with a coloured certificate to prove it!

After leaving Hood, Frank joined Valiant and got married in Warwick before departing for a spell of duty in the China Station where they sailed 1,000 miles up the great River Yangste. He left the Navy in the mid-1930s and during the Second World War worked in a factory supervising the manufacture of machinery parts for use in The Invasion. Continuing in this sphere, he ran his own business until 1955 when he retired and moved to Hatch End.

Frank's second wife, Margaret, whom he married in 1969, has also been a talented and versatile sportswoman whose achievements in table tennis, golf and bowls have won her considerable acclaim and many awards.

The late Frank Hiorns (1900-1999).

In a feature published in the All Sport and Leisure Monthly for September 1993, the reporter Graham Sharpe wrote: 'Sport has been the driving force behind both Frank and Margaret's lengthy and active lives and it is noticeable that they still make a perfectly matched mixed doubles team'.

Another writer, Audrey Moxham, published an oral history account of an interview with Frank in September 1997 and reported that 'his recipes for living to such a great age, at the same time remaining active, are: not smoking since 1935, eating cornflakes, porridge and walnuts every day and drinking Guinness, Scotch, Brandy, and/or Gin every day (without ever being drunk!)' She added 'May you have a happy 100th birthday Frank'.

Sadly, unlike Bill Stone, Frank didn't quite make it to the century as he died in December 1999 but at the time of his death, he was the oldest member of the Association. His name and many achievements will live on and it's good to know that a number of his medals and other naval treasures, including the Crossing the Line Certificate, are in safe-keeping at the Royal Naval Museum, Portsmouth. It is also good to know that his widow Margaret continues to maintain contact with the Hood Association.

HARRY CUTLER'S NAVAL MEMORIES
Hood service: 1922-1924

Harry was born in May 1905 at Woodlands, Dorset, and joined the Navy in February 1921. He was sent to HMS Impregnable at Plymouth and after just a year of rigorous training, was ready to go to sea as a 'Boy First Class'.

He joined Hood in June 1922 and found going to sea an unforgettable experience. Although they visited several harbours during exercises with the Home Fleet, he was not allowed ashore while 'still a boy'. Harry's brief account of their trip to Brazil (for Independence celebrations) includes a jubilant reference to his first shore-going experience when invited to tea at the British Community in Rio with a group of his companions. He was also lucky enough to play cricket with a Boys' team in Jamaica on their way home in December. During the goodwill tour to Scandinavia in May, he had been made an Ordinary Seaman and was able to 'go ashore unsupervised', but had to be back on board by the 10pm boat. When at Oslo, he went on a sightseeing tour, but missed the last boat and was punished accordingly.

In company with all his fellow shipmates, Harry regarded Hood's famous World Cruise as the highlight of his Naval career.

Naturally enough, his most poignant memories centre on trips ashore and the many exotic points of call and sightseeing with friends and relatives.

When in Sierra Leone, he had a train ride into the jungle and through friends he made at Cape Town saw much more than he would have on his own. By the time they reached Perth, Western Australia, Harry was an Able Seaman and presumably allowed more latitude because he and a friend stayed with a couple overnight in that lovely city and even went to a free cinema.

In Melbourne, he was amazed to meet some old friends of his father's who had emigrated in 1894. He was also lucky enough to be driven round Sydney and had a day out at the Races, as invitations with free entrance tickets had been given to the ship. Harry says that 'I came away slightly better off than when I went in. But have not been to a Race Meeting since'.

Thanks to his Melbourne contacts, Harry was given an introduction to a relative in Auckland, New Zealand. That kind man then took Harry with two pals on some wonderful drives, whenever they could get away. They were even taken to the famous hot springs off North Island which Harry had glimpsed on film years before in Wimborne, Dorset.

On the next lap of their historic trip, they were welcomed by the natives of Fiji who had never 'seen a sight like the Hood'; tested their balance surfing in Honolulu; were given a warm welcome in Vancouver; and were treated to a grand dance in San Francisco.

Like other shipmates, including Bill Stone, Harry was astonished by the engineering feat involved in Hood's passage through the Panama Canal.

Their last few visits were to Halifax where they played cricket, Quebec, 'a place of real historical interest' and to Topsail Bay, Newfoundland - their last port of call.

In return for the hospitality they all received in almost every harbour throughout the world, Harry says that he and all Hood's crew were only too pleased to show their many visitors round the ship whenever the opportunity arose. Above all, he remembers the cruise as a wonderful way to 'show the flag' to the then British Empire.

During his next twenty years in the Navy, Harry served in a variety of ships that provided extensive experience and progressive upgrading.

Having endured a range of challenging duties, Harry also survived the war years relatively unscathed.

Back at the Devonport Naval Barracks in July 1945 he left the Navy in a civilian suit after 24 years and eight months of unbroken service.

HOOD'S PICKET BOATS
Recalled by Capt. GEORGE BLUNDELL
Hood Service: 1923-1924

According to this unusual graphic account, Captain B was fortunate enough to be a Midshipman of one of Hood's two picket boats from May 1923 - Oct 1924, a period that included the World Cruise.

In view of an American sailor's description of Hood as 'a mighty fine picket boat' (described by Gunner 'Windy' Breeze), it is perhaps appropriate that Capt. B should honour the role of her two steam picket boats' crews with such accolade.

Each of her 'oil-fired 50 footers had a double crew of one Midshipman, one Petty Officer Coxswain, two Able Seaman Bowmen, one Able Seaman Sternsheetsman, one Stoker Petty Officer for the engine room and one stoker for the boiler room.

'At the time one did not give it a thought, but, looking back, their competence and loyalty were incredible. Not once during the whole of my time did my boat run out of fuel, fail to have steam immediately after being hoisted out, fail to carry out the whole trip ordered on leaving the boat, or not be manned speedily by the proper crew. On the 'World Cruise', when in harbour, the two picket boats ran almost continuously the whole day, the early boat mooring up at midnight and the late boat at 2am or later'.

As Capt. B learned to his cost, the large propeller was right-handed and because stern power was equal to ahead power, the stopping power was enormous, so that when going astern or coming alongside, the stern could kick quite viciously to port. A good stoker Petty Officer was therefore invaluable when docking in the right place. As Capt B says 'The crew backed one up marvellously - they provided all the thrill of a closely knit and trusting team'.

A Hood picket boat in Portsmouth Harbour.

One of his most searing memories is the occasion when they were taking some officers from Hood alongside the detached mole at Gib. to land at Flagstaff steps. He badly misjudged the going alongside manoeuvre and ran the bow firmly on the submerged bottom stone platform of the steps. 'Being the senior officers in the boat, the three commanders, looking somewhat shaken, made to land over the bow. In ringing tones I sang out 'Nobody is to leave the boat'. I then ordered my passengers, including the three commanders, to stand on the stern sheet gratings. As the officers of commanders' rank appeared somewhat hesitant at carrying out my order to stand on the stern, perhaps I was over-peremptory with them. However, the stern went down and the bow rose up and the crew were able to right the boat's precarious attitude. Much relieved, I sang out 'Carry on ashore'. I can see the faces of my three commanders now. The engineer looked very angry, the paymaster non-plussed, but the PMO (pudding) was beaming. In due course I was reported for insolence, my leave was stopped and I received a dozen from the sub. (Punishment was applied whilst bending over the ejector pipe from the sump in the subordinate officers' bathroom).

The stoppage of leave hurt me most because my uncle, a Captain with the Gibraltar garrison artillery, was taking me out to dinner at the Bristol and to a performance of The Pirates of Penzance. Two days later, my divisional officer, A M Carrie, a submariner doing his big ship time, and the snotties nurse, H H McWilliam, an unusually quiet and capable gunnery specialist invited me to spend the evening ashore with them and to see The Pirates. (Carrie, whom I worshipped, was lost when M1 was sunk off Portland)'.

Among other disasters, Captain B described one at Freetown, Sierra Leone, when they were anchored in Destruction Bay - so named due to treacherously strong currents. One evening he was taking the first picket boat up to the boat rope on the starboard lower boom but overshot the mark. The boat suddenly rose on a huge swell, catching the funnel in the boom and causing it to snap off at its base. It was saved from going over board by its 'after guys' but the Commander, whose cabin was nearby, came out and stopped the poor culprit's leave until the funnel was restored.

The way in which remedial help was accorded the poor unfortunate, typifies the spirit of goodwill prevailing in Hood. In Captain B's words: 'I was very ashamed but my dear coxswain and stoker PO helped me hoist it up onto the boat deck where we lugged it along to the coppersmith's caboose. It was in the First Watch but he came straight up from his mess and was so sorry for this penitent Midshipman that he sat up all night brazing, welding and hammering the severed funnel back on its base. By 'Place Spit Kids' time next forenoon the funnel was all back and the boat running in the afternoon. That shipwright seemed to me a very old and fatherly man whose kindness I shall never forget. In fact, ships' companies of those days seemed nearly always kind and sympathetic to the 'middies'. Perhaps they saw in them a kindred 'depressed class' - what in today's language would be called 'under-privileged'.

A further disaster befell the unfortunate 'Middie' at Singapore when, after a hectic morning of non-stop 'relay', he was told to collect the Bishop of Malaya who was in a hurry.

Within reach of Hood, the harassed 'Middie' spotted a large, white yacht-like steam vessel sliding round the stern. As this vessel was covered in awnings, festooned with assorted flags and tassels and had a number of passengers in spotless white, lounging on the deck, he surmised it was yet another 'goofing party'.

In accordance with the 'rule of the road', she should have given way to Hood and the intrepid 'Middie' forced her to do so. The big yacht had to go full astern therefore, as the picket boat slid alongside to embark the precious Bishop, to the accompaniment of 'a terrible din'. He then saw the yacht recover her dignity and also slide majestically, alongside with saluting guns firing and bugles sounding. As he lay off, waiting, in some trepidation, he learned that the Governor of Malaya was paying an official visit to Admiral Sir Frederick Field, accompanied by the Sultan of Johore. He could only gasp: 'Oh merciful oblivion, draw a veil over my subsequent fate'!

And he survived to tell the tale, to have his life saved at Albany, South Australia by a quick-thinking Bowman.

He was sitting in the gun-room smoking when he heard the call, 'Away first picket boat, at the double'. So he thrust his pipe into his monkey jacket pocket and tumbled into the boat with the crew following.

As they set off for Suva, he saw one of the Bowmen face aft to house his boat hook and then, without any orders, he had a bucket of sea water emptied over him! His immediate reaction was 'Help, Mutiny!' but then he saw his Bowman grinning and heard him say: 'Sorry Sir, but you was on fire'! the Coxswain standing beside the 'Middie' had not seen his pocket burst into flame. But fortunately, as a good seaman, the Bowman acted quickly.

Captain Blundell's reminiscences ended with this tribute to Petty Officers:

'I have often reflected on what a lot of the Petty Officers tactfully taught me on how to behave. One day we landed a number of officers just after lunch; the ship's company was still at work. On return I asked the coxswain 'What do the men think of the officers going ashore in working hours?' Jeff looked at me with that 'three badge' twinkle in his eye. 'Lord, bless you Sir', he replied. 'We likes to see them out of the way'. I have never forgotten that wise remark.'

MEMORIES OF THE MUTINY AT INVERGORDON
Commander ALEXANDER F. PATERSON
Hood service: 1930-1932

Like his brother Ron, the Hood Association Chaplain, Alexander was trained as a Boy Sailor. But being several years older, he entered the Navy in 1928 and his journal is the only one in this book containing an account of the famous, unprecedented Mutiny.

He was drafted to Hood as an Able Seaman in 1930 when she was in the Atlantic Fleet. They all looked forward to their autumn cruise and assembled at Invergordon in the Cromarty Firth to commence eight weeks of strenuous competitive exercises and sports. Instead, as he wrote: 'None of this was to happen because the Atlantic Fleet mutinied. The ships refused the Admiral's orders to go to sea. No blood was shed but it was a passive resistance to obey orders until the injustice of reducing low pay even further, was rectified'.

As history reveals, most strike action, whether peaceful or violent, is prompted by economic deprivation and inequality and the Invergordon Mutiny was no exception. The scene was set when an economic committee reported to the Labour Government under Ramsay Macdonald the urgent need for drastic savings of 170 million pounds and recommended pay cuts for teachers, police and the armed forces. When the Cabinet rejected such cuts, a coalition Government was formed to rescue the country from the brink of an unprecedented catastrophe. One of the first acts was to impose a tariff on all imports. Then followed pay cuts.

Alexander wrote: 'In 1931 the five Sea Lords, all Admirals, known as the Board of the Admiralty, were so out of touch with the ordinary matelot that it failed to appreciate the delicate task of informing the navy that in the National interest, pay cuts were essential'. Due either to an oversight, or just bad timing, news of the reductions did not reach the lower ranks until the Fleet was assembled at Invergordon. It was announced that the wages of the lower paid ratings were to be reduced by 25 per cent. This meant that for an Able Seaman, the backbone of the Navy, his meagre pay of 4 shillings a day was cut to 3 shillings with much smaller cuts for the officers.

Alex Paterson whilst a Lieutenant-Commander.

As soon as the news had been assimilated 'below deck', inflammatory speeches began in the canteen and a voluble leader Able Seaman Wincott 'pleaded for the cuts to be restored, describing them as the forerunner of tragedy, misery and immorality among the sailors' families.' When the Officer in charge of the Naval Patrol was prevented from entering the canteen to investigate the trouble, he reported the situation to Flagship Hood.

Alexander distinctly remembered hearing groups of sailors singing the 'Red Flag' but no-one who had not been with them could 'understand what had happened to cause such unusual behaviour'.

The next morning, all was revealed.

It had evidently been decided that at 06.00 hours, instead of following the usual routine to 'Fall in and clean ship', every lower deck sailor should muster and start cheering in succession, to support each other, starting with HMS Rodney.

This state of passive resistance continued for two days with a total disregard for any orders. Unlike strikes in recent times, there were no threats of violence against those who did not want to join in. (The few in this category included Alexander because he had set his sites on promotion.)

When on the second day, Rear Admiral Tomkinson decided to break the deadlock by ordering all ships to raise steam and proceed to sea, none of the stokers reported to duty so the stale-mate was maintained.

Rumour had it that the Admiral flew to London to convince the Admiralty that the Atlantic Fleet would not go to sea until the pay cuts had been revised. At any rate, later that day, a signal reached all ships: ' The Admiralty has decided that ships should return at once to their home ports where each individual case of hardship will be investigated. All fleet exercises are cancelled. Ships to proceed independently'.

Aboard Hood, this was followed by the Captain addressing the ship's company and recommending they should comply with the Admiral's injunction. But when he withdrew, his place was taken by one of the mutiny leaders who explained that only by remaining in harbour could they achieve their objective. In Alexander's words: 'Once at sea and separated, the cause would be lost. He called for a show of hands to decide. Every hand was raised in favour of remaining in harbour except four of which I was one. Somehow or other, I could not disobey an order but then I had little to lose in comparison with those sailors who had their own homes and families.'

When the order to 'Prepare for sea; cable party on the foc'le was broadcast', Alexander therefore joined Cable Officer Lieut. Commander Langley Cook. Instead of the customary party of twenty, they were the only two and what they saw showed it would be impossible to weigh anchor because every cable had been securely lashed with heavy wire. And so the Mutiny continued.

After four days however, there were signs of lessening tension. First, the Admiralty announced a date for completion of their investigations and their decision to reduce the proposed cuts to ten per cent. Secondly, the fact that the Admiralty signal stated that ships were to proceed independently, provided a loophole for those not in favour of continuing in harbour when there was an offer to go home.

Thus, the deadlock was broken and the passive resistance 'Mutiny' petered out. But it had shaken the world's admiration of British power to such an extent that within four days the Government was forced to take sterling off the gold standard.

Within the Navy, there were also far-reaching consequences. The First Sea Lord was not censured; Rear Admiral Tomkinson was placed on the retired list and four other Admirals who had been directly involved, were not re-employed at the end of their current appointments. Six Captains were also relieved of their commands, three hundred and ninety seven sailors were discharged and the chief 'ringleader' Able Seaman Wincott left the Navy to join the Communist Party. When he went to Russia to help run an International Seamen's Club, he spent ten years instead, in one of Stalin's Siberian Labour Camps. During his fifty years of voluntary exile, he still retained a deep affection for England and the Navy and when he died at the age of 75, his third Russian wife arranged for his ashes to be scattered in Plymouth Sound.

To conclude this episode in Naval history, Alexander wrote: 'The final analysis of the true loyalties of the ordinary British lower deck sailor to his country should make us all reflect that within a decade nearly half of those who took part in the Invergordon Mutiny had been killed defending the Empire.'

After Christmas leave, the reconciled fleet resumed its normal programme and Hood enjoyed visiting the West Indies. Alexander wrote: ' At Nevis the attraction is still to visit the tiny church where our Lord Nelson was married. But we were all glad to escape from the heat and return to Portsmouth'.

(According to Ron Paterson who has kindly provided the relevant pages from his brother's autobiography, Alexander's life in the Navy continued with 'A normal career as a Naval Officer rising to Captain's rank and retiring after 31 years' service. As he had held the rank of Acting Captain for less than three years when he was head of a Naval Commission in Turkey, he reverted to the rank of Commander on retirement. Sadly, Alexander died recently on 4 June, aged 90, but practically all the family was present for his Funeral Service, conducted, most appropriately by his younger brother Ron).

JAMES EDWARDS

Hood service: 1933-1934

James started his Naval career at HMS Ganges and served in Hood from September 1933 - August 1934. He started as a Boy First Class but became an Ordinary Seaman on his 18th birthday in February 1934. Having survived the War, he remained in the Navy until 1956 but Hood always had a very special place in his heart because it was his first ship and a very happy one.

James always spoke very highly of Commander Rory O'Conor and the pride everyone took in the appearance of the ship as well as themselves - due in no small measure to the example that was set.

When he first started his training as Right Centre Sight Setter in 'B' Turret, he was dreadfully sick but learned to overcome the condition, as most sailors do, although he found the boat deck most restorative!

James recalled his first trip to Gibraltar for Spring manoeuvres when they were out in a Force 8 gale for steaming trials in company with World War 1 battleships and about 8 destroyers.

He said: 'One by one, each of the destroyers had to give in and ask permission to return to harbour. As this was not granted, they moved into the lee of the larger ships for some protection. The destroyer Windsor was next to Hood and we felt rather sorry for the men'.

James was evidently surprised if not a little dismayed, when his next draft was to Windsor!

Once they had reached the safety of Gibraltar and able to go ashore, James found his land legs again and remembered having to 'walk up the Rock' as there was no cable car in those days.

Painting ship at Gibraltar.
The entire crew of the 'Mighty Hood' took the greatest pride in her appearance.
The paintwork was maintained to a mirror finish in peacetime.

James became a Member of the Hood Association in the seventies and was proud to march to the Services held at Portsmouth and as his ancestors came from Boldre in the New Forest, he and his family always enjoyed the annual Memorial Service there. Sadly, James died in 1996 but his daughter Patricia who has kindly contributed her father's memories, recorded his comments on the news of Hood's sinking: ' I was in a pub and had just ordered a pint of beer when the news came over the radio and the pub went totally quiet. I looked at my pint and could no longer face it, so I walked out, leaving it untouched on the bar. I had lost friends and companions but above all, I had lost the beautiful ship which gave me my first real sea-going experience and I felt shattered.'

HOOD, THE SPRINGBOARD TO A NOTABLE CAREER

Vice Admiral SIR LOUIS LE BAILLY KBE, CB, OBE, DL

Part One: Initiation   1932 - 1933

In the course of an extremely successful and varied career, Sir Louis spent a total of over three years in Hood. His first period of service, as a cadet straight from Dartmouth, was at a most formative period of his life and it shaped his entire future. His informative and entertaining book The Man Around the Engine, contains a fascinating account of his 'initiation'. He says: 'From the moment we reported to the officer of the Watch, the whole rhythm of life was a boy's dream come true. From 0600 when we slipped out of our hammocks for PT, arms drill or polishing the huge brass stove in the Sub-Lieutenant's end of the gunroom until ten in the evening, we rarely stopped or wanted to. Always we were learning.'

The lighter side a Naval life a game of deck hockey aboard Hood bound for Gibraltar for Spring exercises 1932. Louis Le Bailly in centre of picture.

The many skills the novices were required to learn included: being alert night and day for the pipe and shrill cry of 'Away picket boat's crew'; how to drive a picket boat through half a gale when returning a group of cheerful officers to the ship late at night; how to take sunsights at noon and starsights at dawn; to keep watch on the hundred yard quarterdeck in harbour and to help run the routine which governed the lives of nearly 1500 men, for ever keeping an eye on the weather and the fleet.

Sir Louis says that 'Even after half a century, incidents from that happy year come to mind. He even survived and can recall, without rancour, an attack of 'searchlight eye' he suffered during a night-time exercise and literally 'deafening' experiments with 'X' turret's 15in. guns when a Midshipman's gun crew became 'guinea pigs'. He says with characteristic candour: 'The six of us selected were nearly blown overboard and the three of us who survived the War, are all deaf!'

After running a picket boat for the whole of the memorable Spring Cruise during 'halycon days' based at Gibraltar in 1933, he became one of two Midshipmen responsible for running Hood's 'singularly unmanoeuvrable drifter HMD Horizon.' Later in the year, he was required to carry out a challenging trip as Horizon's navigator with one of the two watchkeepers, under a young Lieutenant. He regards that somewhat stressful voyage as 'a milestone signalling the end of a sea-man's career and the start of another which initially, I viewed with distaste'.

Even before leaving Dartmouth, one of his eyes had 'shown signs of falling below the hawkish vision needed in those pre-radar days.' When a further test confirmed this diagnosis, he was told that if he stayed in the Navy it would have to be as a paymaster or engineer. Fortunately, Captain Binney, who had been on the selection board when Louis entered Dartmouth and then joined Hood at about the same time, gave him some sound advice: 'Engineers have to place in the hands of those who fight the Naval battle the most effective weapons that the state of the art can achieve and then go into battle with those weapons and keep them operational as long as they are needed. Mobility is by no means the least though perhaps the oldest of these weapons. Do you not think that it is worth staying in the Navy that I know you love, to sharpen and help wield it?'

Sir Louis says 'Few Midshipmen had wiser counsel' and consequently, he spent the next three years at the RN Engineering College known as Keyham. When, duly qualified, he joined Hood again as a Sub-Lieutenant.

Part Two: Life Below the Waterline 1937 - 1939

The young engineer's journey from dockyard to 'the great assembly of ships for the Coronation Review in 1937' awakened emotions that had lain dormant during the Keyham years. He says: 'Here once more was the Navy and a ship I knew and loved. To rejoin a ship and work below deck after fifteen months in the same ship as a very small cog in the world of executive command, was a major turning point in my life.'

He was relieved to find many familiar features unchanged and even his cabin, 'a small hutch' below the armoured belt, opened onto a flat' where he had once slung his hammock.

In his new role as a Lieutenant (E), he was one of an impressive, experienced team consisting of 10 qualified engineers, 8 watch-keepers, of whom 4 were also Lieutenants (E), plus 3 warrant engineers, (ex artificers) and one warrant mechanician - all indispensable. There were many others of equal calibre, including Chief Stoker Watson who had started when Hood was first commissioned and was the only man to have visited he 1,000 watertight compartments, and Chief Stoker Abbott who watched paternally over all 300 stokers.

'Thanks to good teachers', according to Louis, he was awarded his engine room watchkeeping certificate in four rather than the normal six months. Perhaps one of the most innovative and successful schemes with which he was associated was the establishment of evening classes for stokers and young artificers, relating their work to the running of the ship.

As a result of these classes, productivity and efficiency in boiler cleaning and operation increased dramatically. Like many others during the same period, such as Association Committee members Nobby Clark and Dick Turner, Sir Louis also recalls some of the varied sea-going and shore based activities that gave them all a refreshing and invigorating glimpses of life above deck.

For light relief, he enjoyed his time as fixtures secretary for the popular stokers' orchestra of harmonica players, known as the 'Hood's Harmony Boys', run by Chief Stoker Cathmoir.

In Malta, a few days before Christmas 1938, they heard the ship would return home early in the New Year for a major refit. It would seem that his administrative efficiency landed him with the entire arrangements for a great paying-off dance in Portsmouth.

Hood's 'Harmony Boys' Louis Le Bailly right centre wearing cap.
The 'Harmony Boys' provided entertainment for the rest of the crew.

From then on until they left Malta early in 1939, Louis spent his time in almost continuous session with the ship's dance committee or ashore in the cable and wireless office. Apparently he found the equation between costs and affordability, a difficult one to solve because the outgoings involved hall hire, a band and refreshments at no more than 2/6d per head! The helpfulness of the Mayor of Portsmouth enabled him to book the lovely old Guildhall, 'one of its last functions before Hitler destroyed it'. Unimaginable at the time, to the organiser and participants, it was also the last social event of Hood's life,

With the dance successfully behind him, Louis was 'allocated to the hackwork of the refit and came to realise Hood's unfitness for war as there were many defects besides her thin deck armour'. As clouds of conflict gathered and war became an increasing certainty,

Louis became painfully aware of the disparity between what had to be done and the 'blazing irrelevancies' the Admiralty poured out. Renowned throughout his distinguished career and in his active retirement, for plain speaking and adherence to his principles, Louis wrote: 'Endless hours were spent cajoling officials torn between instincts and orders'.

Sub-Lieutenant Louis Le Bailly 1936.

When they sailed for war, six months later, 'all Portsmouth and Southsea turned out to cheer farewell to a great ship, one they would never see again.' On the fateful 3rd September, they had just left Scapa Flow and were in the North Atlantic when the start of World War Two was announced. Louis recalled: 'I was on watch in the great cathedral of Hood's forward controlling engine room when a messenger brought me the signal 'Total Germany' which meant 'Commence hostilities'. A few hours later, the Athenia, with many children among her passengers, was sunk by a U-boat. Then came the signal, 'Winston is back', to encourage us all.'

Hood's champion rifle team 1935; centre left Hood's Captain Thomas (Big Tom) Tower and right centre her Commander Rory O'Conor.

By then, Louis had been offered an appointment to the battleship King George V but in the interim became Hood's upper deck damage control officer. He saw action for the first time when Hood was struck by a bomb in the North Sea during the rescue of submarine Spearfish.

Before they returned to the relative safety of Scapa Flow, routine tests revealed a critical contamination of the boiler feed water. As a result, some vital tubes and tube joints failed and could have caused a severe dose of 'condenseritis' had it not been for an ingenious application of 'first aid to plug the leaks'. The substance used - surprisingly but successfully - was sawdust fortunately available from the shipwrights.

Having reached Scapa Flow safely, they met another snag due to inadequate space between the tube plates and outer casing. Lacking any robot midgets, their only solution was to send their smallest artificer, the unfortunate ERA Wigfall, into the worst condenser to tighten the joints and plug the leaking tubes. Louis recalled that the poor, intrepid man was fortified for 24 hours with frequent draughts of 'Shovril', a restorative blend of Sherry and Bovril with the former increased to combat his growing exhaustion! When he

125

was finally prised from the small manhole, his lips were blue and his teeth chattering but he had the distinction of saving Hood from possible disaster. Thanks to his labours, she remained at sea but with reduced maximum speed.

During October, in the worst possible weather, 'continuous rolling and pitching caused the deck joints to leak so badly that running water on the messdecks added to the miseries of extreme cold and overcrowding. Constant pounding tired the old hull even more than the ship's company, boiler cleaning became never-ending and machinery maintenance increased daily. Louis maintained that 'In Grogan the Chief and Erskine the Senior, we had superlative leaders who for another six months kept the ship at sea until the work that should have been completed was put in hand.' With his usual candour, he said: 'Dartmouth had instilled into me that what the Admiralty said or did was always right. Now I came to realise they were often entirely wrong. It was the start of a lengthy awakening.'

October 8th was a very special day for all the ship's company because they were visited by Churchill and Grogan evidently told him about the sawdust solution to their condenser problems.

After sorties in October and early November when Hood was en route for Devonport, Louis received a signal ordering him to report to Newcastle. It was a sad day for him when he left Hood, the 'springboard' to his career, but he realised it was time for him to move away from so many happier and easier days.

Seventeen months late in April 1941, when serving in HMS Naiad, close to Hood in Scapa Flow, he was invited aboard by the Midshipmen for whose engineering instruction he had been responsible, to celebrate their promotion. After a convivial visit to the gunroom he was invited to supper and found about a dozen of his old friends waiting to say 'goodbye'. In less than six weeks, they were all dead.

'Running A Big Ship, on Ten Commandments'

By Rory O'Conor, Commander of Hood
1933-1936

News of Rory's appointment to 'Mighty Hood' as Executive Commander in 1933 was a cause for great celebration by his family and many friends and the next three years undoubtedly represented the most memorable highlight in his career.

Hood was at Portsmouth for a refit in the summer of 1933 and although Rory had expected to join her 'on re-commissioning' in July, there was some delay in the Dockyard schedule. An unexpected breathing space of a few weeks gave him time to prepare for his demanding new role especially as he was accommodated at the Victory Barracks nearby.

According to a Naval Manual 'The Executive Officer is next in importance to the Captain. He is appointed to carry out executive duties in the ship and is responsible to the Captain for the fighting efficiency of the ship, the general organisation and routine of the ship's company and the discipline, morale and welfare of everyone on board .....In the event of the death or incapacity of the Captain, the command of the ship devolves upon the senior surviving officer of the seaman branch.' No wonder even with the experience gained by a senior officer, some preparation time for such a daunting 'job specification' would be welcome.

Rory had already demonstrated his gift for leadership, his organising ability and concern for general welfare. Now he could look forward to extending his sphere of responsibility with the authority to put some of his beliefs into practise. While his loyalty to the Service and adherence to its code of discipline were paramount, he thought the way a ship's 'code of practice' was expressed in written form left a lot to be desired.

His previous experience of sizeable ships, Prince of Wales, Barham, Royal Sovereign, Resolution and Emerald, convinced him that simple, concise directions, like signals, were more readily understood and followed than long, elaborate ones. He also believed implicitly in a man's inalienable 'right to be heard', if the need arose, irrespective of rank. While awaiting the commencement of Hood's new Commission, he had plenty of time to formulate and crystallise these ideas. They were embodied in his famous 'Ten Commandments', which were launched in Hood and also laid the foundations for his notable book.

The ship was eventually ready for occupation by late August. Once all the new crew were aboard and the initial process of settling in had been completed, the entire Ship's Company was assembled on the Quarter Deck. The great moment for the new Commander's debut had arrived. Vice-Admiral Sir Louis Le Bailly provides an eloquent account of the occasion: 'I suppose the greatest impact was when he tore up the voluminous Standing Orders and substituted his own "Ten Commandments". Their introduction to the new Ship's Company was dramatic. There was what we called in those days a Magic Lantern on the Quarter Deck and the ten were put on one by one as he explained their relevance. Then almost from a puff of smoke, Admiral Sir John Kelly, so beloved by the sailor, appeared from the after hatchway and gave a stirring address.'

To what extent this genie - like manifestation was stage-managed can only be surmised. The charismatic Admiral - at that time C in C of Portsmouth - was renowned for his unconventional 'short-cuts' and as Rory was also regarded as quite a 'showman', the two had much in common.

Owing to further delay in the Dockyard, Hood was not pronounced ready for sea-going until early September. This interim period provided a good opportunity for the company to become well-established, to get to know fellow messmates and above all, to assimilate their 'Ten Commandments'. Rory's Hood Album - now reposing in The Royal Naval Museum, Portsmouth, is an unusual and possibly, invaluable personal Log. In addition to copies of some official signals, letters, press cuttings etc., there is a fascinating miscellany of personal memorabilia including a series of original poems composed by a resident, if anonymous bard. These compositions record, in ballad-like form, the most memorable highlights (and even some of the 'low-lights'), in the first part of Hood's spectacular 1933 - 36 Commission.

The first, dated 30 August 1933, conveys the poet's graphic impressions at the start of a new Commission.

The breakers beat with gentle friction
On many a league of sunlit sand,
And softly, like a benediction,
The seventh heat wave rules the land.

And gaily, on the golden beaches,
The masses bathe and eat their grub;
While lovely blondes, with skins like peaches,
Bask at the Portsmouth Swimming Club.

Spent are the world's primeval forces,
Her parliaments are in recess;
The dog days run their idle curses;
The news is barren in the press.

In this comatose condition
A living thunderbolt is hurled -
The day has come to recommission
The Largest warship in the world!

The pipe is sounding and the bugle
And orders ringing out amain;
The wardroom, scorning to be frugal,
Is celebrating with champagne;

And on the messdecks is a humming
That swells at times into a roar,
Old messmates gone and new ones coming,
"Old ships" connecting up once more.

Then bang the drums, our show has started,
It is a grand and splendid thing,
Nor mourn the ones who have departed -
The King is dead, long live the King.

Within a week (that is, provided
The Dockyard let us sally forth)
The greatest flagship will have glided
Far out to sea, towards the North.

The bard's next poem, written on 6 September, commemorated the departure for Scotland of that 'most colossal warship', much to the relief of all aboard.

AUTUMN CRUISE AIRS

No Sail (Air 'The flies crawled up the window')

The sun burned in the heaven,
No cloud was in the sky,
I rose at half-past seven
And gave a joyful cry.

On seashore and on high land
Beat down the violet rays,
The roof-tops on the Island
Swam in a gentle haze.

Selecting a clean collar,
I could not help but laugh -
We leave the dockyard squalor
For two months and a half.

The Palace and the Plaza,
The Fawcett and the Goat,
And other spots where bars are,
Too numerous to quote.

We travel where no fuss is,
No panic and no heat,
To where the bright blue buses
Depart for Princes' Street.

Thank God, it was not dirty,
The sea had not increased;
We sailed at 1330
And headed for the east.

Goodbye to just one more ship
Ho! Promulgate it forth,
This most colossal warship
Is sailing for the North!

SUNDAY 11th MARCH, 1934

The day was long, the waves were high,
The Quarterdeck was far from dry.
The force controlled by A.C.Q.
Made slowly for the rendezvous
To meet the vessels of force 'A'
But when we reached it, where were they?

We sought them with binoculars,
With telescopes and Zeisses,
And scanned the clouds with Barr and Stroud's
And similar devices;
But no success repaid our toil,
We could not find Sir William Boyle!

The breakers bursting, swift and strong,
Were watched by an admiring throng
But it was not so pleasant for
Destroyers of the Commodore,
Maintaining, with embittered smiles,
AV/S touch for 80 miles ...

And in a score of Spotting Tops
In many different classes,
Each Captain stood in fiery mood
Re-focusing his glasses,
Till ships became so tempest tossed
That even V/S touch was lost .....

MONDAY, 12th MARCH

The waves are shooting through the air
And washing down the guns;
The weight of water everywhere
One hundred thousand tons;
The Admiral's office is awash,
The messdecks flooded out;
And seaboots and a macintosh
I would not be without! ....
Where has Sir William Fisher gone
Though wireless sparks are dead,
We've got a D/F bearing on
Some warships of the Red;
But visibility is bad,
We do not want to fight,
And everybody will be glad
To have a peaceful night.

Roll on, roll on, a day of rest,
How excellent it sounds!
(The bookstall damage is assessed
At over fifty pounds).
Past troubles will seem very light,
Forgotten all our toil,
The day we actually sight
Sir William Henry Boyle!

Following her spell of time in home waters, Hood's first destination in the New Year was Madeira. Judging by the contents of the resident 'bard's' last poem, he and the Editor of 'Chough', Hood's regular publication, were both being replaced.

The Chough
VENTIS   SECUNDIS

H.M.S. HOOD   **NO. 7**   **JANUARY 1935**

The Editor has changed again,
And one by one our artists leave us;
But still with willing seat and strain
The happy task proceeds amain
Till others shall relieve us.
So welcome this, the SEVENTH CHOUGH,
Of whom no voice has cried 'Enough!'

The Christmas leave has gone once more,
And, like a vista stretched before us,
There looms MADEIRA'S sunny shore,
Which HOOD has visited before
And praised in happy chorus.
Again we see Gibraltar's peaches
And VILLAGARCIA'S barren beaches.

Contrary to her company's expectations, Hood was heading for an unfortunate and totally unpredictable event that caused widespread publicity and extensive repercussions.

Rory O'Conor on Hood's Quarter Deck.

CHAPTER FOUR

Mariners' Memories
Through The Years 1934-1941

T.H. (TOM) CROPP
Hood service: 1934-1936

After twelve months rigorous training at St Vincent, Gosport, Tom joined Hood as a Boy 1st Class, at Portsmouth, in November 1934. He says: 'What a massive sight greeted us Boys as we lugged our kit on board! I think it took us at least a fortnight to find our way around that mighty warship'. Tom recalls that his main job was as a messenger. Without a tannoy system in those days, he had to be always on the alert for the 'Bosun's whistle' transmission of orders.

He has a vivid memory of the 1935 Spring manoeuvres that engaged the Mediterranean and Home Fleets in a demanding 'mock war' involving tricky situations such as rescuing 'a man overboard' and disentangling vicious wire hawsers from protruding oil and water pipes. Following the unfortunate collision between Hood and Renown, their programme was interrupted by the need to return to Portsmouth for repairs. He says they made up for lost time when they returned to Gibraltar with intensive inter-Fleet sports that usually resulted in Hood 'Topping up her showcase with trophies'.

During some 'courtesy calls' on the way home, Tom remembers being at Funchal in the Canary Isles when there was a bread strike and the ship's bakers had to work overtime to supply the Embassy and British residents with bread and cakes!

In a totally different change of scene, he also remembers having to man the pump for a diving party in the 'beautiful clear waters of Scapa Flow' and he compares the stream-lined suits worn by 'Frogmen' today with the heavy, cumbersome equipment available for divers in Hood days.

*A Hood diver is lowered over the side to ascertain the extent
of damage caused by the collision with the Battlecruiser HMS Renown.*

Tom can also recall the spectacular Fleet Review for the Silver
Jubilee of King George V and Queen Mary in July 1935 and says:
'What a wonderful sight it was when warships of all the Navies
in the world stretched out along the length of the Solent. Then
at night, thousands of onlookers lined Portsdown Hill to see the
illuminations'.

During 1936, Tom was a messenger in the Commander's office at
the time that Commander Rory O'Conor was assembling material
for his famous book 'Running a Big Ship On Ten Commandments'.
He says that Rory O'Conor, whom they all respected, helped to
make Hood the outstanding ship in the Home Fleet and made a
lasting name for himself in the memorable commission of 1933-1936.

Tom left Hood in August 1936 after nearly two years aboard but
says it was not the last time he saw her. When he was in Barham
at Liverpool for repairs, following torpedo damage off Iceland in
December 1940, he went aboard his old ship with a group, to
relieve some of her crew for a week's leave. During that week he
noted that 'Hood was badly in need of rest and repair'. Sadly, it
was to be his last contact with his much-loved old ship. Luckily for
him, he survived the later sinking of Barham and has lived to tell
the tale and share his reminiscences.

During May 1936 the deposed Emperor of Abyssinia,
Haile Selassie visited Hood at Gibraltar.

STANLEY JAMES (JIM) HASKELL
Hood Service: 1934-1938

Jim Haskell served in Hood from 1934, just after the Spring Cruise, until nearly four years later, in 1938. He joined as a 2nd Class Stoker, in time progressed to a Stoker 1st Class and, of course, 'overlapped' for a while with 'Nobby' Clark whom he remembers well.

He has several vivid memories of those happy years, many of them centred on his contact with Commander Rory O'Conor whose prodigious 'photographic' memory impressed so many. It would appear that in addition to learning the names of the entire contemporary crew, the Commander could even recall them away from the ship, months later.

According to Jim, 'A three badge Stoker, with First World War medals, had left Hood for almost a year when he met the Commander ashore in Queen Street. He saluted him but after walking for about five yards, heard a shout 'Plowman'. He turned and found the Commander waiting to speak to him. He had remembered his name after all that time.

137

Returning to his own experience, Jim recalls his first morning aboard when he and other new arrivals were sent into the Commander's cabin for individual interviews. 'He wanted to know where we came from etc. and then said 'Have you read my Ten Commandments? If not, do so and you will never be in trouble if you follow them' How right he was!'

He had another clear memory of an unusual incident in 1935 when they went to Las Palmas as a break from Gib. and found when they arrived that the tugs were all on strike. 'So Captain Tower, with the Commander's help, took the ship into harbour, turned round and berthed alongside, using just our engines - a marvellous feat'.

The for the whole of their time there only the Duty Watch remained on board so that the rest could bask on the beaches ashore. Unfortunately, they had hadn't realised that although the sky appeared to be hazy, they could still be sunburnt and there was evidently a long queue of burned and blistered sailors requiring treatment at Sick Bay when they returned to the ship!

Jim also remembers that when a messmate, Mickey McClure transferred to Subs., he considered following his example and sought an interview with the Commander. He says: 'I can see him now. He leaned on the desk and talked to me like a father: 'How old are you? Have you ever been on a Sub?' Then he said: 'You are only young yet. Take a look at a Sub. and if in a year's time, you are still in the same mind, I will grant your request.' When Jim visited his friend in 'Salmon' and saw how they lived in a Sub, he thanked the Commander for his advice and asked for his request to be withdrawn.

On another occasion when they were tied up along the coaling jetty at Gib. and Jim was an auxiliary Watchkeeper he was sitting reading when he realised the Commander was approaching, obviously dressed for dinner. Jim went to stand up but says: 'He just motioned me to stay put and came and sat beside me and chatted away until he said: 'I'd better get back or there will be no dinner for me'.

Jim sums up his feelings about service in Hood with this pertinent statement: 'To me Hood was always my Navy, the finest ship I ever served in'. As a corollary, Jim also avows that another lasting effect of his time in Hood was the number of enduring friendships it engendered. While most of his other Naval friendships were quite casual and tended to last only for the duration of a Commission, 'Hood friends endured for life'.

For example, during 1933 when training in Portsmouth, he met a lad called Eric Price who came from Alderley Edge, Cheshire, while he was from Dorset. But after they joined Hood in 1934, they frequently 'spent weekend and sometimes, seasonal leaves in each other's homes' and in 1935, they even met their respective future wives while they were together.

Later, he palled up with two other Stokers, Frank Thompson, known as 'Tomo' and 'Yorky' Hayes but still continued to maintain contact with his original friend Eric. And the friendships didn't end there because when they all married, around the same time, their wives also made friends! Even when they were all separated by various postings, they all continued to correspond and to meet whenever circumstances permitted.

Jim reckons that some of these friendships forged in Hood, lasted for up to fifty years. Sadly, he is now on his own but says he is sustained by his memories.

N. H. COOMBER
Hood service: 1937-1938

Mr. Coomber is another ex-sailor who served in Hood during the mid-thirties, from 1935 to 1937, as an Engine Room Artificer. He remembers that when they were in the Mediterranean with the Home Fleet in 1936, they were supposed to be coming home for Christmas but 'It was not to be'. Instead, they went to Las Palmas and were given shore leave whenever possible, to offset the disappointment. While there, he bartered for 'a very fine cane chair which was brought home in Hood, is still in good condition and a much-cherished memento'.

WILLIAM (BILL) CASS
Hood Service: 1938-1940

Bill served in Hood from September 1938 to June 1940 when his job as 'S.D.O.' Messenger often gave him advance information about what was going on. He says that he frequently handled signals such as: 'Raise steam for 28 knots and proceed' and whatever the weather conditions, Hood did just that, sometimes crashing her way through heavy seas.' This was sometimes too much for the destroyer screen as he recalls:

'There was an occasion when one of the modern destroyers dropped astern with structural damage and later re-joined our screen with the signal ' I have now shored up and am as seaworthy as a V and W.' (The V and Ws were First World War destroyers, not very glamorous but first-class sea-boats')

Bill's service in Hood must have corresponded with other Members of the Association but in such a large ship, as others have pointed out, any kind of socialising was confined to those within the same section and duty area.

Guide dog 'Hood'.

At about the same time, that the Aquitania and Hood were both in Gibraltar, during late September 1939, Bill's brother died and was buried in the Isle of Wight. But, owing to the critical international situation, compassionate leave could not be granted.

He recalls another Island connection with a pal known as A.B. Patsy Ogan who lost the sight of one eye during Hood's war-time action at Mers El Kebir. When Bill was on leave later, from HMS Sandwich, he visited Patsy while he was convalescing in Ryde Hospital.

It so happens that since Bill's retirement, he has raised funds for several charities including Guide Dogs for the Blind and is pleased to say that one of his ten dogs was given the distinguished name of 'Hood'.

THOMAS KEITH EVANS (Commander, Retired)
Hood Service: 1938-1939

Born in September 1919, Keith was educated at Pangbourne College. He entered the Navy in 1937 and joined Hood in January 1938 at Palma, Majorca and left in January 1939 when she was in Malta.

Although he was only aboard for a relatively short period, he had an extremely active and happy year. It is clear from his reminiscences that Hood's impact on him at such a formative time in his young life, was considerable and far-reaching.

Like so many others, his experience in Hood helped to shape his career and generated life-long friendships. Keith's recollections of his challenging and varied year are spiced with numerous anecdotes and also reveal an unusually good memory for names.

When he joined as a Pay-Master Cadet, on a warm, sunny day, he was met by Paymaster Lieutenant Geoffrey Henderson, the Captain's secretary and within half an hour, he was playing deck hockey! (One of many popular Keep Fit activities.)

He can also still remember Chief Writer Jones, Petty Officer Morgan who was a good footballer and Leading Writer Gatrell in the Captain's office, from whom he learned a lot. During his training, he spent some time in the ship's office, in pursuit of his Ledger Certificate; in the Stores as a Victualling Officer; in the Galley, making bread and rolls and as a wine caterer in the Gunroom where Gin was only 3d. a tot!

Keith's personal memories of Mediterranean ports and harbours are also informative and often enlightening. While based in Gibraltar, he remembers the Combined Fleet manoeuvres for their vast array of ships, the many sporting and social events and the effect of the Munich crisis in 1938. Like Association Treasurer Nobby Clark who was in Hood at the same time, he also recalls the week they were in Gibraltar, spent in close proximity with the German pocket battleship Deutschland and their reciprocal visits.

Keith Evans, taken in Valletta, Malta.

While off the coast of Spain during the same anxious period, he describes the occasion when Hood took on board refugees from Barcelona and Valencia who had come from Madrid to join up with Franco and disembarked at Marseilles. This episode had more personal meaning for him perhaps because he and CPO Writer Jones took down particulars of their passengers as they came aboard.

An on-shore outing to Tangier with his special friend Frank Hearn, had unfortunate and memorable consequences. Having visited some of the local 'flesh pots' in extreme heat, they decided to cool off with a ride but got hopelessly lost. As a result they were so late and looking very scruffy, they had to share a boat taking local dignatories to a Reception on board. When the Paymaster Commander spotted them at the top of the gangway, with nowhere to hide, he was extremely angry and they were given 'seven days No.11' as a punishment.

They evidently survived, somewhat chastened and Frank and he formed such a lasting friendship that it extended to include their respective families and continued for many years after their Naval days until Frank's sudden death in 1993.

Of all their 'ports of call', Malta became Keith's favourite both in Hood days and throughout his Naval career even when there were some unexpected intruders. For instance when Hood was in the floating dock at Palatorio Grand Harbour for ten days' minor repairs, he and the other 'Snotties' slept on camp beds in the Junior Officers' Club and the place was full of noisy cockroaches. They overcame their disgust by lining up the intruders for races between the beds!

Keith also remembers the more traditional and energetic sporting activities that were available such as racing, tennis, cricket, squash at the Marsa and hockey at the Corradino. He became very fond of Malta and the Maltese people as did his mother whose remains lie in a casket at the bottom of the Grand Harbour.

During the rest of Keith's time at sea, he served in many ships and reckons that he led 'a charmed life' because three of his subsequent ships were sunk after he left them.

On the 24th May 1941, he was serving in HMS Hawkins as Captain's secretary when on the tannoy of another ship they heard the announcement of Hood's devastating loss. Keith relates: 'All hands on deck seemed to stop what they were doing for about a minute. As a former shipmate, I just could not comprehend that the 'Mighty Hood' had gone and I am not a bit ashamed to say that I began to cry'.

FREDERICK CONNORTON
Hood Service: 1939-1940

As a Royal Navy Reservist, Fred served as an A.B. in the summer of 1939, cruising around Scotland in the motor yacht Shemara. When War seemed imminent, they hastened back to Southampton and he went home to Portsmouth for the weekend. Almost immediately, he received a telegram instructing him to report to his depot and within days, he was back in Scottish waters, attached to the Mighty Hood. He remembers being awestruck by the vast quarterdeck as he and other draftees were guided to their quarters by 'seasoned regulars' who made good-natured jibes about their possible potential.

Following the declaration of War on Sunday 3rd of September, they were soon underway and on patrol in the North Sea with frequent practises in Action Stations procedure. Fred was assigned to a magazine 'down below', loading shells onto the lift and remembers the Warrant Officer instructor warning them about the accuracy of German gunfire which he had experienced at the Battle of Jutland in the first World War. When one of the lads asked: 'What happens Sir, if we get hit down here?', the reply was hardly reassuring: 'The Royal Marine Sentry ensures that the hatch is shut and floods the magazine'. Not surprisingly, Fred was relieved when he was transferred to an upper deck loader because he thought: 'If it comes to the push, I could always jump overboard'.

He then recalls his first experience of 'Action Stations for real' in late September when the Ark Royal was damaged and Hood received minor injuries - thus giving the iniquitous Lord Haw Haw a chance to exaggerate.

An October highlight was the visit by the First Lord of the Admiralty, Winston Churchill, while they were anchored at Loch

Ewe. When their distinguished visitor left the ship, after addressing the ship's company on the quarterdeck, he was given three cheers as his launch drew away. Fred noticed that Churchill waved a handkerchief in reply but as he turned to enter the cabin, he dabbed his eyes.

At home on leave for Christmas, Fred was recalled after only four days and rejoined Hood at Plymouth. During the first two months of 1940, when they were engaged in extensive patrol duties in northern waters, they were assailed by heavy seas and Fred recalls being fascinated by seeing the vast quarterdeck submerged by massive waves.

As many of the key gunnery ratings had failed to return to the ship in time for her sudden departure, many 'rookies' including Fred had to take their places. Fred remembers being inside a 15 inch turret and having to pull a lever to bring a one-ton shell up into place behind the huge breech and says: 'I felt sorry for the Lieutenant Commander in charge when he dropped his head in despair as he tried to lick us into shape'.

At the end of January, Fred was cleaning the Admiral's barge when he was informed he'd been offered a draft to the Gunnery School at Whale Island. Although he was reluctant to leave Hood, he accepted in order to gain some qualifications.

Crossing London in May 1941, he saw the sinking of Hood Headlines and thought about those poor men at their Action Stations below deck with horror and overwhelming pity.

HOWARD DENIS SPENCE
Hood Service: 1940-1941

A Charmed Life on the Ocean Wave: Memories of a Very Able Seaman

Howard was born in Portsmouth and had a Naval father who served in HMS Hampshire during the first World War and was lucky enough to leave just before her final voyage when she was sunk with Lord Kitchener on board.

Howard joined Hood as an ordinary seaman at Plymouth in May 1940 and recalls the names of many memorable shipmates such as Jon Pertwee, Ian Seraillier, author of the Silver Sword, Edwards grandson of the Archbishop of Wales, and many other fine lads such as 'Lofty' Bonner, 'Mad' Grey, 'Young' Coote, 'Ginger' Fitch, 'Boy' Clayton, A B Miles, R R Gillichan, 'Honest' Thomo, the Librarian, Christian Brau of the Free French Navy and 'Nobby' Ball who got married on his final leave.

After convoy work in northern waters, they heard the sad news of the fall of France in June 1940 and went to Gibraltar. Given shore leave, Howard joined 'a seething mass of sailors, soldiers and airmen and refugees fighting each other' who had evidently had too many drinks in local bars. The next thing he remembers was being dumped in a picket boat and then falling asleep on board Hood. When awoken by crashes, gunfire and explosions, he staggered to the upper deck to join his fellow loaders in the 4' AA gun crew and was warned by his mates of trouble due to an Italian air raid. Later, he was reprimanded by CPO Sheppard who kindly spared him from inclusion in the Commander's Report in order not to influence a forthcoming 'promotion board' unfavourably. But Howard was warned 'not to be so stupid in the future'.

He then recalls the tragic destruction of the French Fleet at Oran in July 1940 when 'one French near miss showered our 4' AA gun with purple dyed water and I thought I had been hit'. The gunfire from both 4' and 15' guns was so deafening, Howard developed tinitus as a 'permanent legacy'.

Back to Scapa Flow and patrol into northern waters early in 1941, they heard the ominous news that Bismarck was at sea.

Fortunately for Howard, about 13 of Hood's crew including Jon Pertwee, were suddenly given chits to go south. He remembers that en-route for Pompey which had been severely bombed, he stopped at a pub near Victoria station in London where he noticed a stocky chap in nondescript clothes. Howard knew him to be a deserter from Hood but neither spoke a word and went their separate ways.

When he arrived home on 24 May, he heard the tragic news of Hood's sinking followed by a Telegram for his parents: 'Regret your son is missing, presumed killed' and then a further one on 29 May: 'Your son not on board, regret anxiety caused'. Howard says 'I have had a life bonus of some 58 years to date for which I thank God'.

WILLIAM HENRY THRING HAWKINS
Hood Service: 1938-1940

Born in Portsmouth in 1923, William admits that he was inspired to join a friend at the Royal Naval School because he was told they had fish and chips twice a week! Following his initial training there in 1938, he was transferred to HMS Vincent for further instruction and believes that 'the long period of training accounts for the fact that we have the finest Navy in the world.

By 1940, after a period of initiation in Belfast and Frobisher, he was drafted to the 'Mighty Hood' as an ordinary seaman. He recalls that daily life in Hood demanded continual training in readiness for action and that his 'station' took a while to master as the watch was in the 'spotting top'. Fetching cocoa in heavy seas was decidedly hazardous and, as everyone aboard discovered, she was wet inside as well as out in bad weather. A 'mopping-up' rota - not exactly popular - had to be maintained day and night.

His 'spotting top' station proved an asset, however, during such action as the immobilisation of French ships at Oran. Then, luckily for him, he left Hood in February 1941 to become an asdic operator in Penelope.

Having survived the war, he terminated his Naval career as a Petty Officer in 1947. Now fully retired, he lives in Australia where he feels that war veterans are far better treated financially than they are in England.

LEONARD CHARLES WILLIAMS
Hood Service: 1936-1941

Leonard (Len) Williams served in Hood for a relatively long time, from the summer of 1936 when he joined as a Seaman Torpedoman until February 1941 when he left as a Petty Officer and was drafted to HMS Vernon.

He therefore experienced life aboard Hood both in peace and war and like others (whose reminiscences are recorded in this book), he recalls the lasting effects of relationships formed when they all lived together 'as a giant family'. Len also had a flair for writing and left a comprehensive journal, remarkable for its clarity, cogency and expression of feeling. It seems fitting therefore, that his moving tributes to an unforgettable ship should form the finale to this Chapter of 'Mariners' Memories'.

Describing what it was like to be a member of that 'giant family', he wrote: 'We knew each other's failings and weaknesses and liked each other in spite of them. We slept in close proximity, in swaying hammocks and even bathed together in the communal bathrooms. In fact, we lived candidly with one another, accepting the rough with the smooth.

This sharing and living together forged a comradeship, which one can never find in civilian life. Nor was the ship ever left out of our lives for everything we did was for her. On our smartness, the way we dressed, in fact, everything we did depended on the ship's efficiency rating in the fleet. She was our constant taskmistress. While we could and often did, call her all the rough names under the sun, when things went wrong, heaven help those, not of our company, who tried to do the same.

This is the team spirit we miss when we leave the Service for it is something very fine. Something which, through countless ages, has scaled the highest mountains, fought and won hopeless battles and has made the Royal Navy the finest influence on international affairs the world has ever seen'.

As Len had been promoted to Leading Seaman for the last few months of his time in Hood, in charge of all the emergency electrical circuits, he described the personal impact of her last few minutes with acute poignancy: 'In view of what happened later, it was heart-breaking to know that no opportunity was given to the ship's company to make use of those safety arrangements. In a tremendous flash, a split second of searing time, Hood was gone, rendering all our efforts null and void. After serving for four and a half years in the ship, I knew every compartment, almost every nut and bolt in her. I can almost picture the terrible scene between

Leonard Williams.

decks when that fatal shell struck. The gigantic sheet of golden cordite flame sweeping through the narrow corridors and passages, incinerating everything in its path. The terrific hot blast, the bursting open of the armoured hull under the colossal pressure and finally the merciful avalanche of the cold sea cleansing the charred and riven wreck and bringing peace to those gallant souls I knew so well. On more than one occasion, I have dreamed this scene and have returned to consciousness with the thought that 'There but for the grace of God, went I'.

Len's feelings are movingly encapsulated in the following Poem:

To a Shipmate

Yours were the stars, the sea, the earth
The soft warm winds, the Northern Lights.
Now your fair substance lies in tidal waters clear,
Trapped in flooded steel for all eternity.

You had your dreams, your youth, your hopes,
Ere ship met ship at dawn off Cape Farewell.
Forever now, your body, washed by northern seas
Shall rest, a priceless jewel in Neptune's crown.

One day, perhaps, a saner world will find your ocean grave,
A torn and riven hull; and wonder at the madness of an age
That squandered youth and brilliance such as yours.

CHAPTER FIVE

That 'Many-Memoried Name'
Hood Relics and Memorials

1. A Treasured Relic: Hood's metal container lid

The only known relic to have survived Hood's destruction is the lid of a metal container, the preservation of which is remarkable.

Washed ashore during the German occupation on the Norwegian Island of Senja in 1942, the original container was found by an elderly couple. Fearing its discovery and possible reprisals, they hid the contents, a pay Ledger and other Service documents, and threw the container back into the sea. The documents evidently remained undiscovered but must have been demolished with the house after the couple's death many years later.

After the War, the lid was washed up into the mouth of a small river on the Island's coast. There it happened to be spotted by a young boy who used it to throw at a passing salmon. No doubt to his astonishment, he scored a direct hit and killed the salmon! When he took his trophies home they were evidently treated as a 'Fisherman's feat' worthy of recording. So, the Hood lid and preserved salmon were mounted on a plaque and hung on a wall in the local Anglers' hut.

Early in 1980, a visiting Norwegian Naval officer happened to spot the trophy and recognising the lid's significance, sent it to the Norwegian Admiralty. They then contacted the M.O.D. in London who decided that as the container had housed Naval documents, the lid should go to HMS Centurion in Gosport.

The following year, this treasured relic was re-mounted on a plaque and officially 'un-veiled' by Ted Briggs. Accompanied by a large picture of the Hood, it remains on permanent display to evoke a host of memories.

2. The R.A.F. Home for Hood Guns on Ascension Island

Thanks to a team of engineers at R.A.F. Ascension Island, two original Hood guns now have pride of place on Cross Hill, overlooking Georgetown. The two 5.5 inch guns that formed part of Hood's secondary armament were removed early in the second World War for the installation of 4 inch anti-aircraft weapons and then shipped out to strengthen the Island's coastal defences.

When the R.A.F. arrived many years later, the historic guns were found to be in a sorry state of neglect. A group of dedicated engineers then came to the rescue and after weeks of hard work in their

Two 5.5 inch guns removed from Hood were mounted on the South Atlantic Island of Ascension. The RAF personnel based there maintain the guns as a tribute to Hood.

off-duty hours - even threatened at one stage by floods that washed away the access road - the guns were restored to their original pristine condition.

According to a feature in the R.A.F. News of December 1984, R.A.F. helps maintain memory of HMS Hood, the guns were then handed over to the Ascension Island Historical Society who said: 'Not only are they a fine reminder of the Island's own fascinating past but also of a great warship'.

3. **Hood Bell in a Belfast Church**

The Sinclair Seamen's Presbyterian Church, Belfast, known as 'The Cathedral in the square', has a long association with its harbour, shipyards and seamen. It is fitting therefore, that they should be the proud owner of a ship's bell belonging to an earlier Hood and presented to them in the early twenties. The 'earlier Hood' was the third in that famous line. Although she in no way equalled her illustrious successor and was permanently de-commissioned just before the First World War, she fulfilled a useful purpose as a 'Block-ship' when she was sunk outside Portland harbour as a deterrent for enemy submarines.

Sea imagery naturally abounds in the Sinclair Seamen's Church records and worship as demonstrated in the Minister's evocation

Bell from an earlier 'Hood' hanging in a Belfast church.

for their souvenir booklet: 'In what Church in our land does the ringing of a bell indicate that divine worship is about to begin?' and when he spoke these comforting words: ' We have an anchor that keeps the soul steadfast and sure while the billows roll, fastened to the rock which cannot move, grounded firm and deep in the Saviour's love'.

4. 'Shadow' of Hood

According to a Press report in the Isle of Wight some years ago, Douglas Hinsley who was a Shanklin Hotelier, had two shadows, 'one reflected his jaunt, bulky figure while the second had sleek lines and followed him around for thirty five years'. The latter was a cabin cruiser called 'Shadow' who had started life as a motor boat built in 1914, to serve with Hood.

'Shadow' of Hood.

She had been replaced by another boat in 1937 but was bought by an R.A.F. officer who was in charge of Air Sea Rescue at Portsmouth for part of the Second World War. Thus, she came into her own and was able to prove her worth at the great Dunkirk evacuation. Later, her owner had her converted to a five-berth cabin cruiser but despite major changes in her superstructure, her original teak hull remained intact.

In July 1956, Doug who was working as an engineer in the Midlands, first set eyes on her and was immediately enamoured. Somehow or other, he managed to scrape together the necessary money for her purchase and five months later, after many weekends of scraping, painting and varnishing, he and his wife's efforts were rewarded by her gleaming appearance.

Once she was deemed fit for action again, they and their son David enjoyed many happy days afloat on the River Severn and exploring the Bristol Channel. Despite strong and changeable tides, Shadow's proud new owners had complete confidence in her seaworthiness as she had been built to Naval specifications.

The Author Nixie Taverner with
'Shadow's' owner Douglas Hinsley.

About ten year years after acquiring Shadow, Doug received a letter from Earl Mountbatten asking if he would be willing to surrender the boat's name as that famous sailor and statesman owned a small fleet of numbered boats all called 'Shadow'. When Doug replied that he would be reluctant to relinquish it because of her links with Hood, the Earl kindly agreed to respect the owner's wishes.

When Doug and his wife Rita - both well-known for their stage career - came to the Island in 1971, to take over the Glenshee Hotel in Shanklin, they were faced with the challenge of bringing Shadow from

Worcester via the exposed water of the Land's End. The four-day trip with David as crew, proved unexpectedly eventful and included battling against a Force Eight gale as they approached the Needles.

Through the years, Shadow was berthed for periods at Wootton, Binfield and Bembridge but after being stripped internally by callous thieves, she was transported to the safety of the Hotel garden. Some years ago when they gave up the Hotel it was divided into two houses, one for themselves and the other for David and his family. But Shadow still remains in the garden as a reminder of her distinguished heritage.

5. Models of Hood
a) Model Maker COLIN VASS

Fortunately for posterity, Hood's power and structural elegance have inspired amateur model-makers throughout the years, to reproduce her in miniature form.

As a result of their creative efforts, there are now a number of real-istic models in various parts of the world. Of all these dedicated craftsmen, one of the most successful and best known in this country is probably Colin Vass who is also an active member of the Hood Association. Colin says that his interest in HMS Hood and model making originated in 1959 when he was 11 years old and like many boys of that time, enjoyed constructing various models from plastic Airfix kits.

He was even ambitious enough to attempt 'powered model aircraft' but when they all crashed, decided to concentrate on less hazardous stationary models of boats!

Starting with small wooden kits he progressed to building models from plans, 'scratch building' as it is called.

In 1964 he attempted, and after considerable time and frustration, completed his first large model of HMS Hood, using card and wood. In company with other models of various warships, his replica of Hood was reconstructed several times as his modelling skills improved.

After Colin married in the mid seventies and raised two children, his model making had to 'take a back seat' until he made a series of new models in 1987, using the new and improved materials then available. Starting with the Bismarck and Prince of Wales, he then did a great deal of painstaking research that led to the production of model Hood in 1995.

Following an invitation to the Association Memorial Service at Boldre in May of that year he and his splendid model made their first public appearance.

Colin them became a member of the Association and since then has continued to make the annual journey to Boldre where the now much travelled model is always on display.

Detail from Colin Vass' beautifully crafted model of Hood showing the Admiral's Quarters.

Colin's industry and creative efforts were rewarded when his model was used by ITN during the filming of their documentary 'The Mighty Hood'.

b) Model Maker DAVID WELDON

David Weldon was born in Manchester in 1943 and when his father's job changed in 1957, moved with his family to Tynemouth.

David's interest in ships was fired by seeing 'The Battle of the River Plate'. He says: 'My Dad told me about the ship that took an unlikely hit down the funnel and blew up. I have been fascinated ever since'.

David Weldon's 9 feet long model of Hood under construction.

David's early fascination with ships led him to collecting photographs, articles and books and then extended to the construction of models, especially of Hood.

He says he has been making 'a scale working model of Hood on and off for over 30 years. It is built in tinplate and brass to a scale of 1/96 showing all the plating and armour and built on frames like the original.'

David's absorbing and creative hobby has been accompanied by an extensive correspondence with fellow enthusiasts from all over the world, seeking advice or information.

Through the years, he has also extended his collection of Hood paintings and drawings and has been a valued member of the Association since 1985.

c) **Model Maker JOHN ANDERSON**

There are undoubtedly many other enthusiastic model makers in different parts of the world whose efforts have not been relayed to the Association.

In this respect the following unusual account is also exceptional because it was relayed to Paul Bevand via e-mail from an American enthusiast.

Sent recently by John Anderson from Redwood City, California, it conveys most expressively the struggles he underwent to achieve his objective, in this case a Radio controlled model of Hood to the scale of 1/72.

According to his cri de coeur (which required a few corrections due to the fact that English is his second language) John had great difficulty in obtaining even the basic information he required:

'The problem I am having is locating pictures of her superstructure. All the close up pictures I can find are prior to her refit in 1939. Also, the drawings I have aren't accurate enough . . I have written to about 8 different agencies in your country . . . I have even written to the British Consulate in San Francisco and they said they would try . . . but NO LUCK. HELP! SOS! My wife is starting to believe I am nuts for building a big ship like this and has raised questions about my sanity! (She even says how are you going to get that thing to the lake. She has no sense of adventure.) Any, and all, assistance is greatly welcome. Thank you'

It was most reassuring to learn that this sad saga had a happy ending and reflected some credit on the Hood Association who must have provided some good advice.

John's exultant e-mail read: 'Just a quick little note to let you and the rest of the Hood Association know that this week I received her propellers from England and her speed controller from Canada. All installed today, even her rudder . . . She sits now awaiting her primer paint to dry and other minor details and she should begin her sea trials next weekend if all goes well. I can hardly contain myself. All of this at a secret location so I can see if what I built actually floats!'

6. Hood's Image Perpetuated in Pub Signs

a) The Mighty Hood at Rodwell, near Weymouth

This Pub was probably the first one to be dedicated to Hood in this country due to its location and connection with Fred White, founder of the Association. When it was so appropriately re-named in the mid seventies, the celebration evening was attended by 'regulars of the house' and about twenty members of the Association.

Admiral Sir John Hamilton had the distinction of pulling the first pint which he did with great aplomb. First, he proposed a toast in memory of the great warship and all who lost their lives in her. Then, in true Naval tradition, he downed a pint in one, thus proving himself 'a true pintathelete!'

The 'Mighty Hood' pub in Weymouth.

To commemorate the occasion, the Association presented their first 'land base' with a series of framed photographs to provide customers with a pictorial history of The Mighty Hood.

Members then continued with their busy weekend programme that included a Commemorative Service at the Royal Naval Air Station on Portland.

b) The Admiral Holland, Banbury

In a 'One Man's Britain' article featuring this unusual Pub, Byron Rogers wrote in the early nineties: 'Yesterday's folk-lore, the lost liveries of the Middle Ages, are fossilised in Pub signs'. and thereby, they become continuing, living reminders of their subjects.

The reason why a Public House depicts ' A ship's towering bows' in an area far from the sea and bears that famous name is that Lancelot Holland spent his boyhood in the locality. He was greatly admired by a contemporary local lad Syd Tyrrell who became a writer known for his classic story of village life in nearby Eydon, 'A Countryman's Tale'.

Being a village 'land-lubber', Syd recalled following Lancelot's sea-going ambitions and progress in the Navy with keen interest and rejoiced when his old friend became an Admiral after years of shore-based posts. Sadly Vice Admiral Lancelot Holland lost his life with Hood in May 1941.

When the local brewery opened the Admiral Holland Pub on the post-War housing estate, many of the locals remembered him when they read the Newspaper accounts of Hood's loss and his old friend Syd wrote: ' I am glad to see that the sailor boy I knew will not be forgotten for many a long day to come and I am hopeful that curious youngsters will ask why the Pub is so named.' (Details of the late Admiral Holland's close family connections with St. John the Baptist Church, Boldre, are given in Chapter One.)

7. 'Flagship Hood' in the Railway Fleet

It is good to know that even if no other ship ever bears HMS

Hood's illustrious name, she was one of the first three locomotives in the Fifty Fund Fleet and continues to operate successfully on several 'excursion lines' throughout the country.

The Fifty Fund was started in 1989 as an attempt to preserve the prestigious Class 50 Locomotives in good working order. All fifty of these locomotives had previously been named after famous Royal Navy ships. In mid 1991, the Fifty Fund shareholders purchased 50035 'Ark Royal' and 50044 'Exeter'. Both have since been overhauled and returned to service on the Severn Valley Railway.

The purchase of '50031 Hood' at the end of 1991 by Fund shareholders Peter and Jean Heys (as mentioned in Chapter Two), led to a productive line of communication with the Hood Association as Peter is now Vice-Chairman and Jean the Secretary.

Rededication of the locomotive 'Hood' at Alresford Station on the 'Watercress Line', Hampshire, by the Reverend Ron Paterson. Padré of the Hood Association. April 1993.

Peter's lifelong experience as a much-travelled engineer, combined with a growing interest in Railway locomotives, promoted this acquisition and provided an energetic hobby as he is the official Engineer to the group and the locomotives need considerable maintenance to keep them operational.

According to the Fund's Prospectus of September 1992, 'Hood' is the flagship of the locomotive fleet at present, attending open days and diesel galas. It has proved itself to be in excellent condition, having worked eight return trips in public service on the Severn Valley Railway over one weekend. Good preventative maintenance should keep the locomotive working for some time, until it too, will receive an overhaul.'

A special ceremony at Alresford Station in April 1993, and featured in the local Press, set the seal on the Association's link with the 'Railway Fleet' at the presentation of the HMS Hood
Crest to adorn the Engine 'midships'. President Ted Briggs who performed the unveiling, was photographed with other members of the Association, outside the station, and with the Group's Chairman Jon Dunster, beside the engine.

The Fifty Fund Bulletin of 1994 - an illustrated, well-produced booklet, reported 'Flagship Hood's work during the year, most favourably. Having undergone several essential repairs and renovations including cleaning and painting, she visited Worksop Open Day, the North Yorkshire Moors Railway and the Midland Railway Centre which involved a lot of travelling. Reporter, Neil Morgan wrote: ' Since August 1991 we have gained a lot of experience, some of it the hard way, but Hood has covered more miles in our care than most other preserved 50s put together so we must be getting something right!'

In August 1998, 'Flagship' Hood hit the headlines again when Peter Heys invited a contingent of Association members for a special tour on the Valley Line in Wales, from Rhymney, to Cardiff, Pontypridd, Abercynon, Merthyr and all the stops in between.

The South Wales Echo, dated 27th August, gave the event excellent coverage with a colour picture of J.R. and Den Finden holding the Standard, accompanied by Dick Turner and Jim Taylor, in front of the Hood engine. Their positive and appreciative comments were all accurately reported and indicated what a success the tour had been, such as Den's who said: 'It is fitting a train should be named after the pride of the British Fleet'.

In their report, a week earlier, the Western Mail emphasised the fact that 'Navy Veterans are all aboard Hood again' and as J.R.

summed up: 'We had a marvellous time and really enjoyed ourselves. It was also important because being pulled by the Hood engine is all part of the remembrance of Hood herself'.

8. Tribute from LEN CLARKE an Old Soldier

Responding to an advance mention about this book in the Portsmouth Evening News, Len felt compelled to write about his early memories of Hood as a retired member of the Armed Forces, if not the Navy. He wrote: 'What a welcome publication your book will be. I am not ex-Navy but a 74 year-old soldier who was always fascinated by the 'Big Ships'. My father took me to Pompey dockyard on Navy Days, in 1935 or 1936 when I was only a boy of 8 or 9 and the entrance fee was just two shillings! We had our dinner on the deck of Nelson and our tea on the deck of Hood. Oh, what memories. The size of those ships was fantastic and those great guns towering over us were, to a lad, gigantic!'

CHAPTER SIX

Stepping Stones to a Living Link:
Hood Stones at Eriboll and the work
of Durness Primary School Children

The Hood Association first heard about a unique memorial in northern Scotland from Alan Joyce, a retired teacher and local resident in the area who has Naval connections and takes a keen interest in the environment. In a letter to J.R. dated 3rd July 1992, he wrote:

'HMS Hood has her name recorded in letters 6 feet in length, picked out in white stones in the heather at the 700 ft. contour on the mountain side above Portnancon on the West side of Loch Eriboll in N.W. Sutherland. Along with the Hood are the following ships, Valiant, Swift, Whirlwind, Normandy, Courageous, Unga, Lucretia, Johanna and H43.

The existence of these names is only known to a small group of mainly elderly local people who are anxious for this area to be cared for and marked with a cairn and suitable inscription at the foot of the mountain on the road to Durness.'

Following an appreciative reply from J.R., Mr Joyce wrote again stressing the need for enlisting the support of official bodies 'to keep the site and names in good order'. He even suggested that to protect the area from possible quarrying, its care should be entrusted to the M.O.D. or War Graves Commission. Sadly, it would seem that even if approaches were made, they elicited little response.

How or when this unusual memorial was constructed cannot be easily ascertained. It can only be assumed it was the work of sailors who made productive use of time ashore when their ships were in northern waters. It is known that Hood visited Eriboll for bombardment practice in June 1934 as Ron Paterson recalls.

A commemorative verse was also written by the ship's 'bard' at the time and is recorded in the original Album compiled by the then Commander, Rory O'Conor and now housed in the Royal Naval Museum, Portsmouth. It should be said perhaps, that most sailors found the Loch too remote for their liking and far removed from the more convivial amenities of Naval ports!

Loch Eriboll to Rosyth

Now the guns have ceased their thunder,
Loudly let the trumpet bray!
From the Loch we part asunder
Nor would many wish to stay.

Hood Field Gun crew ashore Loch Eriboll Scotland 1934

It is more than likely that further visits were made later especially as Scapa Flow was their principle northern base in peace and war. In fact, the last glimpse anyone at a shore base had of Hood was at Scapa Flow just before her fatal engagement with Bismarck.

It is probably true to say that the date of the stones' original installation is less important than the fact that their re-discovery generated so much interest among local residents and inspired Durness Primary School to carry out a remarkable, ongoing preservation project.

The high level of communication they have sustained throughout the last eight years matches their enthusiasm and reflects great credit on Head Teacher Graham Bruce and his staff.

Correspondence between Durness School and the Association began when two children Allan Mackenzie and Rowan Van Muysen wrote several well-constructed, informative letters between September 1993 and June 1994 informing J.R. of their progress.

In the first, they said: 'We hope to create, with the help of the Durness Community Council, a picnic site with an information plaque to tell visitors about the Loch and ships.' They also asked for photos and information about Hood and details of any survivors.

Their second letter contained the good news that the project was already attracting some Press publicity and in the third, they acknowledged the photo of a Hood model sent by the Association and said they had worked out the size of Hood but found it 'hard to imagine just how big she was'.

Allan and Rowan's second letter conveyed the good news that the previous day 'the whole school climbed the hill above Loch Eriboll and painted the stones which spell out Hood so they can now be seen across the road'. They also expressed their gratitude for all the interesting information they had received about the ship and said that as they were going on to Secondary School, their places, as correspondents would be taken by others.

The first letter, dated October 2nd 1995, from their successors David Bruce, Sam Bose, Shaun Stephenson and Fiona Miller, sparkled with the exciting report of a Royal visit:

'We are writing to tell you that Prince Charles stopped to look at Hood on the hill above Loch Eriboll when he visited north west Sutherland last week. He had been told how we had repainted the

Children from Durness School around the stones forming the 'H' of Hood.

stones and he talked to Mr. Bruce about it. Mr. Bruce had lunch with Prince Charles in the Cape Wrath Hotel in Durness. We talked to Prince Charles when he visited the new Health Centre next to our school. The children in Primary 7 are writing to Prince Charles to tell him about our investigations into the Hood and other ship names at Loch Eriboll.

This was followed by an interesting letter from the Headmaster who said the visit had prompted him to put pen to paper. He went on to say; 'His Royal Highness was very interested in the Hood name and the part the children played in restoring and publicising it. He was also interested to learn of the Hood Association and that Ted Briggs, as a survivor, was still in the forefront. Along with the children's letter to the Prince, I enclosed a copy of your last Newsletter so you may hear from him.'

It was good to hear from the two school correspondents Angela Ure and Fiona Miller in April 1998, that the Durness Community Council were planning a path from a car park below the Hood stones enabling visitors to see them. A commemorative plaque was also being planned. Writing on behalf of all the Primary School children, they thanked the Association for 'the wonderful picture of 'The Mighty Hood' which would be framed and hung in the corridor for all to see.

A panoramic view of the full 'Hood' stones.

They also described an interesting trip the preceding autumn to Invergordon on the Cromarty Firth to see HMS Sutherland, then the Navy's latest ship, when they were there they talked about Hood and 'tried to imagine what it was like when she visited Cromarty'.

Writing in October 1999, Julie MacLellan, Eilidh Veitch and Lorraine described their recent outing to repaint the Hood stones 'with all the school, even the little ones'. Apparently, the Navy, local decorators and some parents provided the paint for the occasion which was 'great fun and really interesting' even if some of the enthusiastic workers got covered in paint too!

They painted the stones 'bright white so people could see them easily' and included some of the other ships.

The expedition was marked by an appreciative feature in the local paper that also praised their efforts in 'preserving and maintaining this solitary memorial.'

Impetus for the School's project has been positively reinforced in the last few years by the support of Mr James Clark, laird and owner of the Eriboll Estate and Church and his wife Julie.

The local community was delighted when the church which had been neglected for years, was splendidly restored by Mr Clark in 1995 to prepare for the wedding - the first held there for fifteen years.

These auspicious developments gave the Hood Association an opportunity for presenting the church with a Memorial Plaque and led to a special Service being held there in May 1997. In his prior

The painting party!

Press Release, James Clark referred to the absence of any official memorial to Hood in Scotland although she frequently visited the area and many of her crew were from North of the Border.

This fact was given prominence in local papers such as the Independent News Magazine for the North, The Press and Journal and Northern Times all of whom featured the Commemorative Service fully and also paid tribute to the efforts of Durness Primary School.

Happily for all concerned, the Service was a great success in every way as reported in a letter to Nobby Clark from James Clark, dated 28 May 1997:

'We had a tremendous turn-out in our little church with many families who had lost relatives in HMS Hood on that fateful day. Many were moved to tears as it was their first chance to 'bury their dead' after 56 years.

We were especially proud to have Mr Edward Goggin representing the Hood Association. He led the plaque unveiling ceremony with Lt Commander Hollis from HMS Sutherland'.

Eriboll Church.

UPDATE: 2001

At the time of writing, it is most heart-warming to know that Hood's influence still lives in Sutherland where Durness children continue the custom started by their predecessors of preserving the ships' stones.

A letter to the Association Treasurer, 'Nobby' Clark, dated 25 May 2001, signed by three pupils, Julie MacLellan, Eilidh Vetch and Lorraine Kay contained a graphic description of their outing to paint the stones:

Yesterday, after we had our lunch, all 31 children in our school, the staff, some parents and pre-school children, the Minister and the countryside ranger went to re-paint the stones. It was a gorgeous, sunny day, ideal for painting the stones.

We had a long, tiring walk up the steep hill, although many of us were excited. When we reached the stones our first job was to scrape the loose paint from the stones which was quite hard to do. We then took it in turns to paint the stones brilliant white. The local painter Donald Mackay, generously donated the paint. It was quite a messy job but we soon got is done.

We then gathered together above the stones and Mr. Bruce and the Minister talked to us. We thought of all the men who died on Hood 60 years ago and those who survived. We sang a Hymn of thanksgiving and then the Minister told us the story of Joshua crossing the River Jordan. Joshua sent twelve men to bring back twelve stones to put them on the hillside to remind them of God. This was like the crew putting the stones on the hillside above Loch Eriboll for us to remember them. We then said a short prayer.

After that we went down the hill to the guesthouse at Portnacon. There, Mrs Black gave us some wonderful food and drinks including a very rich chocolate cake and apple pastries! Portnacon is where the Loch Eriboll pier used to be. It was here that the sailors from the ships in the Loch would land. You can see all the ship names from there. We really enjoyed our afternoon out.'

It was good too, to hear from the Headmaster Graham Bruce that he had received a letter dated 6 June 2001, from Rodney Gale who lives in Amalinda, South Africa, about his personal Hood connections and complimenting the children. He wrote:

"A few days ago was the 60th Anniversary of the sinking of HMS Hood in which my eldest brother was killed. The battle between Hood and Bismarck is marked all over the world, including here at East London, South Africa.

Another brother who lives in Leamington, England, faxed me today to tell me that the children of your school are maintaining the stone above Eriboll which commemorate Hood.

I would like to take this opportunity to thank all of you at Durness who give of your time and effort to remember that fine ship.

We were four brothers who all served in the Royal Navy, myself not very far away from you at the Royal Naval Air Station, Lossiemouth.

Do please thank the children for us and read this letter to them."

All concerned with the preservation of such a special, unusual memorial, should feel justifiably pleased their efforts are now so widely renowned.   With the present and next generation in mind, it is perhaps, appropriate that some of the children's own words complete this Chapter.   It is worth recording that all the young writers are in the Primary age group of 8 - 11 years old.

PAINTING and PONDERING
Durness School Children's Original Reflections
June 2001
H.M.S. Hood

It was Wednesday afternoon in the year 1999. We were doing our project on World War Two . We came across a bit on H.M.S. Hood. That struck my interest. I was shocked to hear how many people died and I cast a few thoughts for the crew. I felt very sorry for the families of the crew. I wonder how they coped with the loss. I shivered with the thought of how those brave men died.

A few weeks later the whole school went to paint the Hood stones above Loch Eriboll. It was a lovely sunny day but there was a cold north wind in it. We painted the stones happily and ate our packed-lunch when Mr. Bruce (our head teacher) noticed some more stones that spelt H43 the name of a British submarine. Mr. Bruce recalled some more stones of other ships so we went looking for them. Just then it started to pour rain so we went round the hill for shelter and by chance we found the stones we were looking for. They spelt Whirlwind and Valliant. The P7's painted them.

I looked at the loch and imagined the great ship there in 1934. I long to meet the one remaining survivor, Ted Briggs. I would like to ask him how frightening it was and how sad he was when his crew -mates died. Even today those stones stand out on the hill beautifully, reminding us of the crewmen who perished.

By
Liam Wood

The Hood Stones

One day last year all 30 children in my school went up the hill by Loch Eriboll to paint the Hood stones. We also painted the submarine H43 and both the ships Valiant and Whirlwind. There was lots of heather covering the rocks so that made it hard for us to find the stones. It was quite cold on the hillside. It started to rain by the time we had finished Hood and H43 so we went to the side of the hill to shelter until the shower was over. Once it was we went back to paint Whirlwind and Valiant. While we were painting the stones I was thinking about all the sailors that lost there lives on HMS Hood. When we were having lunch I was looking at Loch Eriboll and imagining what it was all like. I think it would be very scary. I am sure everybody enjoyed painting the stones because I definitely did. I would love to meet the one survivor named Ted Brigs. If I ever meet him I would love to ask him what life was like on HMS Hood was like. I would ask him what kind of food they ate and lots of other things like that. I would ask him if he liked the experience of being on a big ship and why he went on Hood. He was a very brave man. I still can't believe that out of 1421 only 3 came back and only 1 is alive today. It would be really interesting if I could meet him.

By
Julie

H.M.S Hood Stones

One fine day the whole school went to a hill above Eriboll. We went up the hill; some of us were carrying white tubs of paint. Others had paintbrushes. When we got up we had to pull all the bracken, grass and heather from around the stones and then started painting. We painted two of then we had our packed lunch.

As I was eating my lunch I was thinking about those brave men who risked their lives for us and how out of 1421, 1418 died and only 3 survived. I really want to meet Ted Briggs the only living survivor .I would like to ask him what it was like in war.

After lunch we did the other ship names. It was hard work. When we had finished we looked at them to see how well we had done.

By Alexander

H.M.S. Hood

One fine day the school went to paint the Hood stones.
They were built by the crew of the huge warship in
1934 when she visited Loch Eriboll.
H.M.S. Hood was sunk by a German ship. There were
1421 crewmen on the ship when it sank and only three
survived. It sank near Greenland.
When I was painting the stones I was thinking of all
the people who died on the ship. I am glad they put
stones there. Now we can always remember the people
who died for us.

By
    Nicola Morrison

Hood Stones

One fine day last year we went up and painted the Hood stones up
the top of a hill. We painted them white. The sailors put them up
on the hill in 1934. There were 1200 on the ship then. In June 1934
she spent 10 days at Loch Eriboll. When we were painting the
stones I was looking down at Loch Eriboll. I thought about the
Hood sinking and the people drowning also the three people who
survived. I felt proud that I was painting the Hood Stones. I think
that the three people who survived were very brave. It was the
Bismark which sank the Hood. Ted Briggs gave our school a
picture of the Hood and it's hanging in our corridor today. I wish I
could meet Ted so I could ask him how they managed to escape.
The stones are still there today on the hillside to make people think
about the Hood.

Alistair.

H.M.S HOOD

One fine day the whole school went to paint Hood stones on a hill above Eriboll. The HMS Hood crew placed stones on the hill spelling out Hood. We thought of the 1418 people that died for us to have a happy life today.

Three people survived when the Hood sunk. They must have been very strong, tough and determined to survive. One person was called Ted Briggs who is still living today .We went to paint the stones so we would have memories of the crew of H.M.S Hood. When we were walking up the hill I was thinking of all the people that died on the Hood. In the middle of eating our lunch I was thinking of all the people who were killed in the war so that we have peace in our country today.

Donna

HMS HOOD

One sunny day we climbed up a hill above Loch Eriboll to get to the Hood stones then we painted them in white paint covering all the bits on the stones. The stones that we painted were put there in 1934 and are still there today. There was 1,421 crewmen on the boat at that time and there was 1419 that died on the ship when it sank in 1941. We were painting other stones too. We made cairns with lots of little stones. They were different stones too. The Hood was sunk on May 24 and the Bismark the German ship was sunk in may 27. We are sitting here now glad that we were not on the ship when it sunk .I still cannot think of all that people that died on the ship. Every time I pass the stones I think of those poor men that died on the ship. But I can think of the ones that did not die .One person is Ted Briggs who is still alive today.

Ashley

The Hood Stones

*One day last year Durness Primary went up a hill beside
my friend's house. We were going to paint the Hood Stones.
It was a beautiful day. We took a couple of pictures up on
the hill. I looked and thought about all of the people that
died. We painted all of the stones bright white. It started
raining for a little while but then it stopped. So we went up
the hill for shelter. We then built a cairn.
I had a great time and I think Ted Briggs is a very lucky
man for surviving. It   probably would have been scary and
terrifying for him. We all got a photo taken at my friend's
house.*

> *By Lorraine*

One fine day all of Durness primary school climbed a hill above loch Eriboll to
paint the hood stones that were there since 1934 when they anchored in
loch Eriboll. I didn't have a clue about the stones or the ship before I was
told. Some people think Eriboll was the last place Hood was before she was
sunk, but it's last place was in scapafloe in Orkney before she was sunk by
the main German ship, The Bismarck , off Greenland. While I was painting
the stones I thought of how she sailed in to the Loch down below and I
would of loved to be on it on that day.

> BY
>
> ROSS

The Hood Stones

*When we went to Laid we all walked up the hill. It was a hard walk. When we all got
up we couldn't find the stones. When we found them we had to pull all the Heather
away. We all had a turn at pulling the heather away after that we all had a turn at
painting the Hood stones. When we finished painting them we had our pack-lunch.
When I was eating my food I was thinking about a wonderful sunny day with the
Hood floating on Loch Eriboll long ago and the sailors walking up the hill and writing
Hood with the stones and still to this day the stones are there.*

> *By*
>
> *Donald*

H.M.S   Hood

As we went down the hill I thought how could 1421 people fit in one boat? We all ran down the hill and waited for our school bus to take us home. If you go passed laid on the side of Loch Eriboll you can see if you look up in the hills you can see our painting. I hope that we can paint the Hood stones again so that people will always think of the brave sailors who fought and died for us.

Calum.

H.M.S.   Hood

One summer's day all of the school went to Loch Eriboll to paint the Hood stones. When the sun came out it reminded me of all those men that died. I could imagine HMS Hood in Loch Eriboll far below. The Bismark struck ammunition on Hoods deck. The hood sunk in about 2 minutes. The Hood came in to Loch Eriboll to shelter from the weather in 1934. Some of the sailors climbed up the hill and near the top wrote the name Hood in stones. We painted the Hood stones bright white so they would show up and people would remember the great ship. There were other names there as well. You can still see them today.

By
David

HMS Hood

When I think of HMS Hood I think about how tragic it was when she sank. Imagine how sad the 1419 wives and families were when they heard about HMS Hood sinking. The three survivors clung together, talking to keep themselves alive, How lucky they were to be on deck and flung clear of the fast sinking ship. Only one of the survivors, Ted Briggs, lives today. HMS Hood was sunk north-west of Iceland in 1941. A few years before, in 1934, the crew climbed up the hill that overlooks Loch Eriboll and wrote in stones "Hood".

For the past 7 years we have been painting the Hood stones and other various ships that came to the loch. I haven't been to paint them myself but my friends have told me that it's really fun. They also told me that they built cairns. I really want to paint the stones. Whenever I stay the night at my friend's house, which overlooks loch Eriboll, I imagine the huge ship anchored there with the sun shining on the loch and rowing boats coming ashore. I wish I knew what it was like on HMS Hood.

Rhiannon Meyer-Turner

The Hood Stones

When we walked up to the Hood Stones to paint them it was a fantastic day. We climbed a big hill. When we got there and started to paint, I thought about the sailors who put them there in 1934. We painted them white. I thought about all the men who died when Hood was sunk by the Germans in 1941. One of the three survivors, Ted Briggs, is still alive today. I wish I could meet him someday because I would like to hear his story. In the school we have a picture of HMS Hood signed by him. When we were sitting on the hill having our lunch I thought it was really sad about all the people who died.

I had a fantastic day painting the stones.

by
Claire

CHAPTER SEVEN

Living Links With Hood's Name

Training Ship Hood: St Austell Sea Cadet Corps

The Corps probably has the longest continuous history of any youth organisation in the country, but like every British institution, it has evolved haphazardly'. This paragraph forms the introduction to a brief history of this long established movement, sent by the present St Austell Unit, Training Ship Hood.

It owes its inception to sailors returning from the Crimean War in 1856 who started a series of 'Naval Lads Brigades'. Originating in Whitstable and one or two other ports, it had extended to several other towns by the turn of the century.

Meanwhile, a 'pressure group' known as 'The Navy League' had been formed in 1895 with the commendable aim of fostering 'maritime thinking' in this country as a reminder of our Island's Naval history and dependence on the sea. The League then decided to sponsor a small number of the independent units by amalgamating them into what became known as 'The Navy League Boys' Naval Brigade'.

By 1914, there were 34 Naval Brigades, which were granted recognition by the Admiralty in 1919, 'subject to an annual efficiency inspection by an officer', and the title 'Navy League Sea Cadets Corps' was adopted.

In 1937, the expansion of the Corps was aided by a grant of £50,000 from Lord Nuffield and at the start of the World War in 1939, there were nearly 100 units containing a total of 10,000 Cadets.

It would seem that war time needs precipitated the next most significant developments because in 1941, the Navy League launched a scheme to train Sea Cadets in T S Bounty for Naval service.

By 1942, the Admiralty had realised the scheme's potential for increasing much needed manpower and arranged for the 'Admiral Commanding Reserves' to take over the training role. Their status was thereby up-graded to the extent that King George VI became Admiral of the Corps, Officers were granted appointments in the RNVR and they were renamed the Sea Cadet Corps. As a result, the Corps quickly extended to a total of 400 Units with 50,000 Cadets. The expansion coincided with 'warship weeks' in many towns that led to each newly formed unit taking the same name as an 'adopted' warship.

The Admiralty took over the costs of providing uniform, equipment, travel and training while the Navy League funded sport and the maintenance of Unit Headquarters. Thousands of 'Bounty Boys' then progressed into the Navy as Communications ratings, many returning to their units after the war. In the same year, the Girls' Naval Training Corps was formed as part of the National Association of Girls' Corps, based mainly in the south of England.

When in 1947, the Admiralty offered to take over completely the Sea Cadet Corps, the Navy League disagreed but suggested that the Admiralty should continue its co-sponsorship of the Sea Cadet Corps as it had throughout the war. A Sea Cadet Council was then set up, incorporating the Navy League and the Royal Navy supervised by a retired Captain. From that time, the Girls' Nautical Training Corps also increased and by the late fifties, contained a total of 50 units.

In 1955, the Sea Cadet Corps was pleased to incorporate a Marine Cadet Section, which quickly expanded from 5 detachments to 40. A few years later, in 1962, the Girls' Nautical Training Corps was eventually affiliated to the Sea Cadet Corps and the combined official base was transferred to Portsmouth under the Commander in Chief Naval Home Command.

At last, in 1980, girl cadets received the full status they earned by being formally admitted to the Sea Cadet Corps, so that by late 1991 over 300 units contained girls.

In 1992, the successful integration of boy and girl Cadets had resulted in both sexes enjoying the same opportunities, insignia, rank, nomenclature and pay.

When they reached their Golden Jubilee year, the Sea Cadet Corps numbered 400 Units, including one in Malta, with a rising total membership of 16,000.

The Sea Cadets HQ has also retained a supervisory role over 3 Units in Bermuda and 1 in the Falkland Islands. Additionally, they maintain friendly links with Commonwealth Corps founded in Canada, Australia, New Zealand, South Africa, Zimbabwe and Hong Kong and others in Sweden, Holland, Belgium, Germany and the USA.

In view of the HMS Hood's connection with West Country ports and the tremendous respect her memory still commands, the St Austell Corps decided to adopt the name when they were formed in 1975 and they became known as 'Little Hood'. Later in the year they gained official recognition by the MOD and were entitled to use the appellation 'T S Hood'.

Meanwhile, Lieutenant Roy Dumbleton, an ex RSM who had spent his boyhood in a Naval College for boys, became a Warrant Officer for Army Cadets. Having lived most of his life in Cornwall, he transferred his allegiance to Sea Cadets in 1978 and became an instructor for T S Hood at St Austell. He took command of the unit in 1983 when Lt-Cmdr Gary Truscott was Sub-Lt and at about that time heard about the Hood Association. Having decided that a link would be mutually beneficial, he made an approach in 1984 to the Hood Association who readily agreed. Thus, a productive 'bonding' was established that has flourished for many years.

According to the few existing Association records of their links with the TS Hood, there were several ceremonial occasions in the eighties and nineties, typified by the one in October 1989 when Committee Members were invited for a special weekend.

A dinner party in honour of the Association was held on Saturday 7 October 1989, at the Porth Avellan Hotel, Carlyon Bay (where their guests were accommodated), and followed by Ceremonial

Divisions on Sunday 8th. Then, at the Sunday Divisions, which followed the best Naval traditions, in every respect, including an Inspection of the Ceremonial Guard, 'Colours' and Prayers, Harry Purdue, then Chairman, presented a Hood plaque to T S Hood. A similar event was also staged on Sunday 22 September 1991 at Charleston Harbour when there was a Parade and Church Service for the 'Laying up of Colours', followed by a march to T S Hood where a reception was held.

Vice-Admiral Sir Louis Le Bailly, inspects the ship's company of 'TS Hood', St. Austell 1988.

One sad occurrence marred the occasion - the sudden death of a guest, Lt Robert Irwin, at a local Guest House. At his wife's wish, his Funeral and Cremation took place locally. Most appropriately, Reverend Desmond Peckett, Chaplain of the Hood Corps, conducted the Service in Kernow Chapel at the Penmount Crematorium, Truro and afterwards, Robert's ashes were scattered there.

1994 was another eventful year in which some special awards were presented to T S Hood by the Association. The first was an Achievement Certificate donated by Mrs A E Jeffs in memory of her brother C P O Surrey who went down with Hood and the second was one of 'knot man' Albert Burton's wonderfully crafted shields donated by James and Joanna Warrand in memory of their father Commander Warrand who also perished with Hood.

During the same period, T S Hood also became the proud owners of a carved wooden Hood crest that had been owned by a resident of Malta who kindly gave it to an Association member on holiday there.

Left: Commander Ian Browne RN presents the HMS Achievement Shield (donated by the Warrand family) to the Commanding Officer of 'TS Hood', Lieutenant G. Truscott, 1994.

In his Commanding Officer's report addressed to the President, Lieutenant Commander Truscott said the year had passed with a mixture of problems and successes. Although staffing levels had been disturbingly low, they had been much improved by the appointment of two most competent female members of staff. Like other Units in Cornwall, they had introduced weekend training programmes that resulted in Cadets obtaining qualifications in Engineering, First Aid, PT and Cookery, to name but a few.

The Unit's boating programme had been very successful with two cadets being awarded a week's cruise aboard the Corps' Flagship'

T S Royalist while 4 others spent a week aboard FT Jonas Hanway, an ocean-going tender run by the Marine Society. They were also grateful to Looe Royal Naval Association who offered to pay for an additional berth aboard the Royalist which would enable 3 Cadets to enjoy a week's cruise each year.

The highlight of the boating season was a week aboard TS Hood, culminating in a sponsored pull from Mevagissey to Fowey. In spite of the fact they were not blessed 'with favouring winds', the pull was carried off in traditional Naval style. After covering some 12 miles, the tired Cadets were still able to enjoy the evening bar-b-que even if some almost fell asleep with buns in hand! Their efforts raised the princely, well deserved sum of £850.

The Commanding Officer was also pleased to report that the MOD had assigned another class to their fleet, an 18ft cabin craft on the lines of an MTB complete with 'flying bridge'.

On behalf of TS Hood, he thanked the Association for the magnificent shield and told them it had been awarded to Cadet Julie Arnold, who had demonstrated such potential and skill on her first voyage to sea, she earned a Special Certificate.

The CO concluded his report by apologising for the fact they had not been free to attend the Association reunion but hoped that he and some of the 'ship's company' would be able to see them the following year when 'Little Hood' would be 21 years old. In recent years, increased travel costs have curtailed reciprocal visits but the link between the Association and T S Hood continues as a reminder of their shared resolve to keep the name alive.

TS Hood's monthly Newsletter, appropriately called 'Hoodlines' always indicates the level and range of activities available to Cadet Corps members. For instance, in the May 1995 edition there were reports of a challenging swimming test; a day of fun collecting in St Austell; a staff training day when a group took turns at navigating a boat up and down river - without mishaps- and the fortitude of 3 drummers who led a V E Day Parade on 6 May and kept going despite such extreme heat that some onlookers fainted.

The July - September issue of 'Hoodlines' featured a profitable Flag Week in which £800 was collected, a Boating Day when they were

Members of the crew of 'TS Hood' in a sponsored 'pull' during 1995

introduced to the new arrival 'Pegasus' and a demanding 15 mile expedition for those wanting to obtain their Duke of Edinburgh Bronze awards.

The District Pulling Regatta in Falmouth proved a great opportunity for female Cadets to prove their superiority if only because they believed their 'team spirit was better than the boys'! Of all the five boats in the race, the boys did well to come fourth, but in the girl's race, they slacked off towards the end and only came second.... They all agreed they needed to do some serious drill practice to prepare for the Drill competition in October.

'Hoodlines' of April 1997 contained some illuminating comments from Cadets giving their reasons for joining the Corps.

Lucy Carter wrote: 'I joined the Sea Cadet Corps when I was twelve and have been coming ever since. The main reason why I joined is because I think it looked interesting. My older brother used to go and I went to watch some of the activities he took part in. Now I have affair amount of badges and enjoy going boating. If I could have more of anything, I think it would be shooting, power boating and sailing. I also can't wait to go to Navy Days. Yippee!'

Arraon Papworth admitted: 'The reason I joined the Cadets was because I was bored at home and was getting into a bit of trouble.

186

So my Dad suggested Sea Cadets . . . I joined and ended up liking it. I enjoy the activities we are involved in. Because it is a disciplined organisation, I got out of trouble and started mixing with the right crowd . . . When you have been in the Cadets you have a better chance of getting a job'.

Christian Collings said: 'I joined the Sea Cadets Corps because I wanted to see what it was like and to learn more about the Royal Navy. In the future I want to do more competitions, sponsored swims and lots of different courses. My ambition is to join the Royal navy'.

Julie Arnold's Poem conveys a salutary reflection on the kind of world we live in. But the dedication and skills of our young 'Living Links' should give us all hope for the future.

In Favour of the Bomb

In a world that's full of hatred,
And news that's mostly bad,
The dividing line gets thinner,
Between who's sane, and who is mad.
If a bloke thinks he's two people,
Is he the useless case?
Or the man that made the bomb
That will destroy the human race?
The ones we think are madmen,
Are in a prison cell,
But the madmen that are ruling,
Are making our world hell!

Should we blindly follow leaders,
And do everything we're told?
And in a war, find that our enemies
Are using weapons we have sold!
We don't care about our weapons,
Whether nuclear, big or small,
But the leaders of our country,
The ones who began it all!

Living Links Overseas

Royal Canadian Cadet Corps 'Hood' - Coboconk

Links between the Hood Association and several overseas organisations have been established at various times, some being maintained for a number of years. Like TS Hood in St Austell, Cornwall, there is a flourishing Cadets Corps in Coboconk, Canada. The original link was forged some years ago by a Canadian member of the Association, Chief Petty Officer George E Donnelly, who had served in Hood from 1936 to 1938. Several Association shipmates who were also in her during that period and whose service is outlined in this book include Dick Turner, Jim Haskell, Len Williams and Vice Admiral Sir Louis Le Bailly. Dick Turner, in fact remembers George well as they were both in Benbow class together.

The only one to whom George referred however, was Sir Louis who, as Lieutenant (E), was his Divisional Officer in the Engine room and for whom he has warm memories.

When George first visited the Corps in 1992, he took some Hood Association Mementos which were much appreciated and he agreed to be the Corps Reviewing Officer at their second annual inspection. The only sad news in that year was the death of Pat Morrow who had served with George in Hood.

In many other respects, 1992 was a bumper year for TS Hood and The Association. The Corps CO, Lt Douglas Melbourne wrote to say they had decided to adopt the Hood motto 'Ventis Secundis' (with favouring winds) and, like their counterpart in St Austell, their total complement of 40 included a high proportion of female cadets. LC Tamara Stuckey, a conscientious and successful high flyer in many areas was one of their star cadets whose efforts were well commended in the local paper. After spending eight years with the Navy League and Sea Cadets, she was one of six to take part in a six week working cruise late in 1992 aboard the Canadian ship Protecteur.

Besides keeping watch for 2 hours each day the cadets worked in the engine room and on the bridge, taking part in all aspects of running the ship. They also had to continue with their schoolwork for several hours each day.

During the trip they sailed south from Halifax to the Panama canal and back up to British Columbia for the ship to be refitted. While they were at sea, it was relatively calm except for two days, but they were evidently able to overcome seasickness sufficiently to enjoy the good food and plenty of ice creams as a welcome antidote to heat around the equator.

Early in 1993 - another year packed with action and success - Tamara also received an award from the Victoria Board of Education for her achievement in overcoming the disability of dyslexia.

Then in June, another press article focused on Cadet Petty Officer Paul Larocque and his Naval aspirations. He outlined his ultimate goal, to command his own ship and said that being a member of the Corps had helped bring his dreams for the future a little closer to becoming true. The Corps had provided valuable opportunities for 'learning the ropes' in every way including summer camps, exchanges and travel, but as a transitional step towards a Naval career, Paul hoped to work as a Civilian instructor after his final inspection at the age of 19.

The July Newsletter contained some interesting news about their summer camp programme and Paul's departure for a 6 week Communications course. At the same time, 3 younger Cadets left for a Junior Leadership course and they all had the honour of travelling on a military plane.

The Hood Association were pleased to hear from the Commanding Officer Lt Melbourne, that the Corps were close to obtaining their own badge after two years of hard work and that George Donnelly had done an admirable job as Reviewing Officer for the Annual Inspection. The Corps conveyed their thanks to the Association for the photographs they had sent to extend the Hood display and plans were under consideration for possible reciprocal visits.

It was also interesting to learn that the Coboconk Corps had welcomed Reverend Ian Taylor and his wife from TS Onslow in

Caloundra, Australia with whom they planned to maintain contact and also with a view perhaps to arranging a return visit.

Lt Melbourne's last Newsletter of the Year contained an account of the change of Command Ceremony as required every three years. He said that SLT Richard Williams would take his place while he became Executive Officer and he expressed the hope that he and his wife Margaret would be able to visit England.

To reinforce the steady and continuing progress of the Corps, they were building a campsite for weekends that catered for everything at Balsam Lake Provincial Park except sailing.

The traditional welcome Christmas Newsletter of 1994 reported that Tamara Stuckey continued to go from strength to strength. She had passed an examination board from promotion to Chief Petty Officer, 2nd Class and at the same time, two other cadets, MacNeil and Dow, had also been promoted.

Another traditional fixture, the Santa Claus Parade had been led by Lt Melbourne who marched as a member of the Legion and at their annual Christmas Dinner, their guest of honour had been George Donnelly who made a gracious and informative speech about his life aboard Hood.

He then presented a special Trophy and ten Achievement Award Certificates on behalf of the Hood Association.

The Trophy, a beautiful shield of knots made by the gifted craftsman Albert Burton, the Association 'knot man' was donated by James Warrand from New South Wales in the name of his father Navigating Officer Commander Warrand who had perished with Hood. The late Mrs Jeffs also of the Hood Association was responsible for the Achievement Certificates in honour of her brother CPO Surrey who lost his life with Hood.

When Albert Burton died the following year, 1995, Lt Melbourne wrote in his letter of condolence to the Hood Association that the trophy he had made for the Corps would be especially welcome. By this time, correspondence between the Hood Association and the Royal Canadian Cadet Corps 'Hood' had extended to a personal exchange of letters between President Ted Briggs and George Donnelly.

In a long and informative letter, George told Ted he would be representing the Royal Navy for the Burlington Memorial Naval week. For the parade they expected up to 1,000 veterans representing the RN, RCNVR and Merchant Navy. The Town Hall would also fly the White Ensign to honour those who fought the Battle of the Atlantic.

Albert Burton the Hood Association's knot expert with the shield he crafted, which was presented to the TS Hood at Coboconk, Canada.

He then explained why such strong Naval traditions and feelings prevail in the Burlington, Oakville and Bronte area. According to local history, the original township of Trafalgar was settled by sailors who had fought with Nelson at that famous Battle and it later incorporated both Oakville and Bronte. Other place names associated with Nelson include the City of Hamilton, the Village of Palermo and Sovereign Street.

The whole areas therefore is quite literally imbued with 'the Nelson touch' and George helped to perpetuate the tradition when he was a Sea Scout Master, by naming their church meeting place 'The Stone Frigate, Sea Scout Ship Victory'.

Ex Hood George Donnelly making a presentation to TS Hood in Canada.

In February 1996 Mrs Margaret Melbourne wrote to tell the Hood Association that after her husband's retirement as C O - a post he had held for six years - she would continue as Administrative Officer, at least until September. She also enclosed a Christmas photograph of male and female cadets wishing all members good health and good luck and said: 'All our Cadets are fully aware of HMS Hood and remember her well as we do'.

Her last letter dated 21 August 2000 proved that she still remained in charge as Acting Civilian Instructor and reported the continuing progress and achievements of their flourishing cadet corps.

Links with Newfoundland and Nova Scotia

One of the best ongoing contacts with these two interesting areas arose from a letter sent to the Association by Dr John Shaw from Dartmouth, Nova Scotia in November 1994, applying for Membership. He said it would be 'a privilege to belong' and that he had Naval connections through his father who served throughout the war. Dr Shaw himself retained his interest in the seas through his work as a marine geologist working at the Bedford Institute of Oceanography and he always spent part of every year at sea.

Writing a few years later, in 1998, Dr Shaw reminded the Association of the past significant connections between Hood and the Island of Newfoundland. He referred to a newspaper article of 1987 recalling the effect the 'Pride of the British Navy' had on local residents during Hood's two-week visit in 1924 as part of the famous 'Empire Cruise'. It was reported that they were all 'in awe of the mighty vessel' and that one visitor, Mr George Williams, had been 'captivated by the floating menagerie that included Joey the Kangaroo'. He was also surprised that many of Hood's sailors were barefooted. The island was no doubt equally memorable to Hood's company especially as it was one of the few places in the world where, in a local football match, the city team beat Hood's by 6-2!

The press article included a picture of a cigarette case bearing raised insignia of HMS Hood. It had been a gift to Island residents from the crew and was later passed to a local resident, Mr Jim Martin of St Johns.

Members of 'TS Hood's' crew. All uniforms carry the crest of HMS Hood.

At the same time, Dr Shaw kindly sent a full list of the sixteen Newfoundland lads who had probably been 'recruited because of the ability to handle small boats' and lost their lives in May 1941.

Thanks mainly to website contact, the majority of those young Canadians are commemorated in both the Roll of Honour and the Memorial Gallery section of this book.

Other Canadian Links
Richmond BC

There was also some contact with the Richmond Branch of the Royal Canadian Legion who wrote to the Association in January 1994 concerning an addition to their 'Honour Wall'. The Veterans' Service Officer, W E Thompson, wrote to say they already had a 16 x 20 inch picture of Hood, with other famous ships but as the display was incomplete without an accompanying crest, they would like to buy one.

The Royal Canadian Naval Association, Burlington

One of the most moving and memorable events of the last decade in that area was the unveiling of the Naval Memorial at Spencer Smith Park on Burlington's lakeshore on Sunday 14 May 1995 during the Royal Canadian Navy week. The completion of this unusual Memorial, the most comprehensive in Canada, was the outcome of considerable planning and fund raising over many years and was clearly worthy of all the efforts involved. It consists of three components, a concrete remembrance cairn covered in 'blue pearl granite' bearing the names of all the Canadian Navy and Merchant Navy Ships lost in the war; atop the cairn a life like bronze statue of a uniformed Naval rating saluting his shipmates and at the back, a large memorial wall engraved with the names of the 527 warships in the Canadian Navy at the time.

The facts and figures incorporated in the Memorial are a salutary reminder of how much is owed to the Commonwealth for it's support and sacrifice in the last world war by Britain and her allies.

According to the facts engraved on the memorial cairn, the Royal Canadian Navy lost 31 ships and 2024 Naval personnel and the Merchant Navy a total of 75 ships and 1,466 seamen.

During the war, the Royal Canadian Navy escorted over 25,000 merchant ships to Britain and convoys to Russia. They also participated in virtually every major sea and 'combined ops' fronts and more than 200 Canadian Naval pilots served with the Royal Navy Fleet Arm.

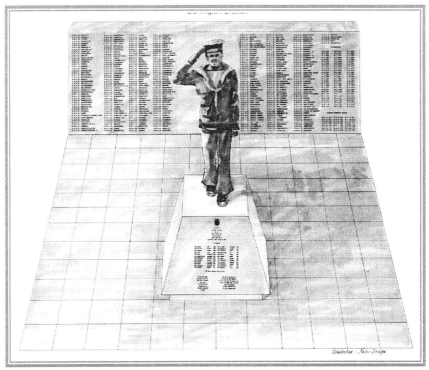

The Canadian Naval Memorial at Burlington facing Lake Ontario.

The ceremony and service also commemorated the 50th anniversary of V E Day and the Battle of the Atlantic and were graphically reported in the June/July edition of The Crows Nest journal published by the Canadian Royal Naval Association, as shown in the following extracts:

'After over a year of work the day finally arrived that we unveiled the Naval Memorial statue and cairn; and what an inspiring sight it was.

The parade mustered on Baldwin St at the High School ready to march off at 1.00pm sharp.'

'Somehow or other, at 13.00 the parade moved off and the veterans showed their stuff. Organised confusion was old hat for them and they marched off with confidence and grand style.'

'At Spencer Smith Park it was evident that the public had also responded for the part was packed with wives and grandparents, children, relatives plus other veterans in wheel chairs who were unable to march.

What a grand sight it was with the refurbished walkway and the green grass and newly leafed trees sparkling in the sun. A perfect setting for the unveiling of the statue, the raising of the 4 permanent flags and the crowd of over 3000 packed together to pay tribute. Sure they were crowded but when you looked around everyone was in a perfect mood and you saw smiles on the children and remembrance on the face of the veterans and one got the sense that every person in the park knew why they were there.

A glorious exhibition of warmth and pride of sacrifices made 50 years ago'.

The compelling poem sent by 'a Senior Newspaper', that appeared in the same feature, epitomises the feelings shared by countless people throughout the world and provides a most fitting conclusion to 'Living Links'.

The Long Watch Keep

Beneath the oceans wild and deep
The Sailors of a nation sleep
For them no crosses row on row
No Skylark's song tumbles from the sky,
To bless the graves in which they lie

Bravely they came from town and countryside.
To launch their ships on the flowing tide.
Now fathoms down beneath the waves,
They lie at rest in unmarked graves.
Today shipmates we pledge our watch to keep
That you may ever in freedom sleep.

By John Virgin

CHAPTER EIGHT

Memorial Service at Hood's Ocean Grave
March 1997

Focal Point of ITN Documentary
'The Mighty Hood'

The way in which such a complex and memorable operation was conceived and synchronised represents a high level of dedication and organisation and reflects great credit on all concerned. Headed by David Mearns, Director of Blue Water Recoveries and ITN Producer Rob White, it was approved by the MOD and had the full backing and active participation of the Hood Association.

As a marine specialist, devoted to wreck discovery and investigation, David has always been interested in how and why ships sink, in the hope that finding the cause can prevent a similar recurrence. Rob's father Captain Robert White was in the Navy for thirty years and had a most distinguished career. It is not surprising therefore that Rob was 'brought up to respect Hood as a wonderful ship' and he might have followed in paternal footsteps were it not for his imperfect eyesight.

Immediately after the broadcast of their highly acclaimed Channel 4 documentary on the exploration of the wreck M V Derbyshire, Rob and David attended an ITN 'get together' in 1995. While there, David turned to Rob and on the spot proposed organising a similar expedition to locate the exact site of Hood's watery grave deep in the North Atlantic. An approach was then made to the Hood Association whose response convinced them of its value and, to set the seal on the project, David and Rob were made 'guests of honour' at the Annual Reunion.

Unfortunately, even before the plans could be finalised an over-anxious Association member got wind of them and assumed, quite incorrectly, it would involve 'desecration of a war grave'. A letter from the British Legion Assistant Secretary to Rob White, dated February 1996, was reassuring and encouraging. He wrote 'A visit to the site where HMS Hood lies would seem entirely appropriate. The British Legion believes it is important that we all remember the consequences of war and it is for this reason that we encourage services at war graves in this country and abroad'. As a result of not being able to raise underwater search funding, the expedition was limited to 'a surface film at the site' but as things turned out, its success - crowned by a moving service - has had far reaching consequences.

The next hurdle was to obtain funding for the project - always a contentious problem, especially as the authorities in this country are less likely to co-operate than those in the USA. This is evidently the reason why so many important maritime programmes are financed by American backers, with the exception perhaps of Channel 4 who have been instrumental in redressing the balance. It seems likely as David suggested, that publicity focused on the Titanic helped to turn the tide in recent years. Viewing figures for recent Channel 4 documentaries have been rewardingly high and indicate the wide interest still sustained by 'this Island race' in all maritime matters. This time, The Discovery Channel in the USA funded the documentary as part of the Battleship series it was running.

The next vital step in the 1997 project was to find a ship suited to the challenging Arctic waters where 'Hood' lies.

Since the British Navy does not operate in those waters, the Royal Danish Navy was contacted with positive results as the Denmark Strait is one of their key operating areas. Both David and Rob agree that Danish involvement in the 'Mighty Hood' venture was a measure of their gratitude to the British for their support in the last World War and because they still regard 'Hood' as a proud symbol of the western fight for freedom.

Having specialised in patrolling and protecting Faroe and Greenland waters for over 400 years, in some of the world's roughest and most freezing seas, Danish ships were ideally suited to the task of locating 'Hood'. The ship selected for the undertaking was HDMS Triton, 'an offshore patrol frigate' of the Thetis class, the second in a series of four and first commissioned in December

1991. Called 'Triton' like many of her predecessors, after the old sea god, son of Poseidon and Amphitrite, the crest had been approved by the King of Denmark in April 1962.

In order to survive the worst severe conditions imaginable, Triton was constructed to the highest technological standards and was even able to proceed through at least 80cm of solid ice. She was also equipped with radar, hull mounted and variable depth sonar, thermal imaging facilities, an integrated command control and communication's system and she carried a Westland Navy Lynx Helicopter. The Triton's internal fittings and living quarters for the crew were also exceptional with well designed store rooms and workshops and cabins described as 'the most luxurious in Naval ships anywhere'.

HMDS Triton.

After months of correspondence and planning (documented in Hood Association archives) the date for the expedition was fixed for 11-16 March 1997 and was marked by Royal approval: 'Her Majesty Queen Margrethe the Second very kindly gave permission for Her Majesty's ship Triton under the command of Commander Svend Madsen to embark the British party of ten on Tuesday 11 March for passage to the Hood grave'. The 'British party of ten' consisted of the ITN Documentary Team, Director Colin Barratt, Producer Rob

White and cameraman Steve Montgomery; two Naval Staff Officers from NATO, Commander Philip Hollihead and Lieutenant Commander Jonathan Worthington and a Royal Marine Bugler Colin Brown plus the Hood Association contingent represented by Vice-President Joanna Warrand (whose father, Navigating Officer Commander Warrand, went down with Hood) and three 'ex-Hoods', Den Finden, Dick Turner and Chaplain Ron Paterson. 'Logs' kept by two of the Hood group, Joanna Warrand and Dick Turner, provide an absorbing account of that remarkable 6 day trip, especially as they differ greatly in length, style and emphasis. Dick Turner's 'Jottings of an ageing Sea-farer' are brief and mainly factual and Joanna Warrand's considerably longer and more anecdotal.

TUESDAY 11th MARCH

They all met at Heathrow on Monday 11th March well ahead of their flight time and left for Reykjavik at 1.45pm. While Dick's 'Log' just records their departure and arrival times, Joanna's contains a vivid description of their airport adventures and the flight. They had taken with them wreaths and posies for the Memorial Service and were relieved to find them carefully handled by airport staff for safe transport in the hold. There was apparently a 'minor flap' however, when Ron discovered he had forgotten his Passport but 'as Iceland Air share facilities with Aer Lingus, no one batted an eyelid at having to make temporary arrangements'. As these entailed going through special customs without a queue, no one objected and Joanna noted that 'Ron looked so angelic and pathetic, a defenceless Padré clutching a wreath and box of ashes' that no one would have had the heart to criticise him!'

Mistakenly thinking that Triton was a 'dry ship', they all stocked up with duty free booze before departure and then enjoyed a comfortable flight in a small aircraft 'with wonderful views in bright sunshine'. On arrival, they were greeted by a snowstorm and Joanna described their hour's drive to Reykjavik in rocky, white terrain, like travelling through 'a lunar landscape'. They had 'a tremendous welcome to the Triton with a guard of honour saluting at the top of the gangway, led by Captain Svend Madsen followed by drinks in the Wardroom' which made them realise their duty free booze was completely superfluous.

Members of the Hood Association and crew member on the bridge of Triton.

The large bridge in Triton also served as a buffet dinning room where according to Dick, they had a 'buffet reception and drinks all evening - a wonderful greeting'. Joanna thought all the food delicious even if she couldn't always identify the ingredients. On a more serious note, they were all touched by the Captain's presentation of a model of the Hood made by a seaman.

Their sleeping accommodation also exceeded their expectations. Dick wrote: 'Finally allocated our quarters. I am sharing ship's sickbay with Commander Phil Hollihead. It's quite palatial with bunks side by side and our own shower room and toilet'. Joanna was equally appreciative, especially as there was 'even a window and CD player'. She added 'The Captain has promised to point out the Halvjiord Fiord where Hood used to go and when Ted Briggs heard about it later, he said: 'We were on our way there, when we were diverted to chase the Bismarck'.

Dick's comments on their first night aboard Triton, were pertinent: 'Slept quite well but awoke during night mind full of thoughts. All so wonderful'.

201

Hood Association Padré Ron Paterson shows a model of Hood, made by a member of Triton crew to the Commander and his guests.

WEDNESDAY 12th MARCH

Their first day at sea started early with a 7am call, followed by a substantial breakfast, then safety procedure for the visitors conducted by the Captain, who recommended extra clothing as they would be exposed to the elements, away from the warmth of the ship.

They had been joined by Elin 'an intrepid Icelandic journalist' who shared Joanna's cabin and provided welcome female company. When out in the rolling seas later, Elin announced 'I feel fine. I just can't stand!' Her reactions were echoed by Joanna who gratefully received a 'seasick patch behind the ear' which made her feel a lot steadier.

A meeting was even held later to discuss the Service scheduled for the following day and Joanna was pleased to learn she would be assisted by a lady from the crew to help drop both their posies into the sea. They were 'also given a little lecture by the film crew on holding them up before dropping them so they could be filmed'.

Dick who spent most of the day on the bridge noted that just as they were running into a snowstorm at 2.30pm, they witnessed the helicopter in action for the ship's lady doctor who was lowered and later picked up by hoist. Joanna joined Dick on the bridge for the afternoon 'bottling up the atmosphere' and marvelling in the breath-taking Icelandic scenery with snow clad cliffs and hills sparkling in brilliant sunshine.

Early in the evening, they had a hymn practice in the Officer's Mess and the Seamen's Cafeteria for the Service the following day. Joanna also noted the superb supper menu with such a delicious dessert that the British Commander on her right had three helpings!

The rest of the evening was spent preparing wreaths for the next day, from the Hood Association, the British Navy, the Ganges, HDMS Triton, the Bismarck and the Ambassador in Iceland. Sadly, the one from the British Legion had arrived after the travellers left London. By this time, they were well into the North Atlantic, proceeding much more slowly and expecting to reach Hood's last known position around midnight. Joanna thought it 'prudent to head off' for her berth, but the indomitable Dick used to night- time watches stayed on the bridge and recorded: '1am, Thursday 13 March. On the bridge over last known position of Hood. Sat with operator carrying out Box 44 sonar search. Sea depth two and a half kilometers plus'. (It was interesting to learn that all radar and Sonar displays on the bridge are in English as it is the common language of technical aids in such ships.)

THURSDAY 13th MARCH

Fortunately, as Joanna noted, the sea was much calmer for the highlight of their trip, the Memorial Service at Hood's ocean grave. All, including the ship's company, mustered on the flight deck at 9.30am for a very special service, most ably conducted - as always - by Hood Association Chaplain Ron Paterson.

Dick read both the most appropriate Bidding Prayer and led the Lord's Prayer before the first hymn 'Thy Kingdom Come, O God'. After his Address, Ron led the familiar Naval Prayer and then, for the most poignant part of a moving service, all the wreaths were committed to the deep, followed by flowers in memory of Commander Warrand by his daughter Joanna, son James and widow Frena.

Padré Ron Paterson conducts a service of remembrance on the afterdeck of Triton.

A cross in memory of Ordinary Signalman Ernest Drury was also committed together with the ashes of Annie Hurst who had asked that her remains should be scattered over the watery grave of her husband Surgeon Commander Henry Hurst.

Special Prayers were then said and as a gesture of respect, every member of Triton's company, led by Commander Svend Madsen, cast a single rose over the side as saluting guns fired three shots. The ever heart-rending 'Last Post' was expertly sounded before the customary silence - accompanied only by the surging of the sea. A stirring Reveille preceded the Naval Hymn 'Eternal Father, Strong to Save' and the Service ended with a Blessing and the lusty singing of both the British and Danish National Anthems, during which standards were lowered.

Having dipped the Hood Association standard, Dick and Den stood together quietly for their own individual prayers and, as promised, said one for Ted Briggs who could not be with them, for medical reasons.

After being interviewed by ITN, they were invited to the lower ratings mess for invigorating mulled Punch and were glad to hear how much the Service had meant to all the sailors and, in turn, that their presence and singing were appreciated. According to Dick's Log entry, weather conditions were 'still a bit choppy' but he thought he'd found his sea legs, or perhaps, just one.

They then steamed north to intercept a German fishing vessel to check it's catch and nets, en route for the pack ice floe. Being able to view the magical scenery from the bridge was an added bonus for Triton's guests. All were affected by the sheer beauty of the glistening landscape, in Joanna's words: 'Lots of lovely shapes, all pristine white like wedding cake icing above the water and greeny blue below'. A wonderful sunset was a fitting end to a truly moving day.

FRIDAY 14th MARCH

After what Dick described 'as a somewhat bumpy night' and Joanna as 'energetic, trying to stay in our bunks', calmer conditions prevailed but only for a while. At one stage, Joanna and Elin's possessions, including pills, were flung all over their cabin and even the chair careered across the floor. A wonderful sunrise, excellent visibility for 10 miles to the horizon, made up for these minor discomforts. Joanna even spotted a seal on the ice, a sighting confirmed by two members of the crew and on radar.

They managed to eat some of yet another delicious lunch and although there was 'a roaring, icy wind, Dick felt he had recovered both sea legs and even contemplated a short 'run in an inflatable' to view Triton from the sea, until discretion proved 'the better part of valour'!

The weather changed dramatically when they left the ice floe and as Joanna wrote: 'The sea went angry green with white crests and huge waves crashing right over the prow and washing the bridge windows.'

Dick recorded that with 'All exercises finished, course was set to 90 degrees, 16-18 knots for home' But the sea ahead was like 'a roller coaster ride'. By dinner time, not even the Captain could stand and it was hardly surprising that some people did not appear for the meal!

Even Joanna had to give up going to the bridge, defeated by the one staircase and heavy doors but noted that in his 'Wardroom', the generous Captain dispensed most of a bottle of brandy - presumably as restorative 'medicinal tots'.

The intrepid ex-sailor Dick must have retained his balance because when a messenger knocked on his door at 00.15 a.m., he got up immediately to see the spectacular Northern Lights and was rewarded by seeing, as well, the 'comet star' Mars and a new moon.

Poor Joanna said she was 'airborne' for quite a bit of the night. 'As Triton dropped down the waves, one rose from one's bunk only to crash back onto it when Triton hit the bottom of the wave.' She added that the 'bumpy ride also makes for interesting meals'. Whereas chairs travelled up and down with the waves, food and drink tended to slide off tables, as down a shute, with the exception of the Captain's table which had some remarkable self-adhering properties!

SATURDAY 15th MARCH

After only three and a half hour's sleep, Dick still managed to go down for breakfast at 7.30 a.m. and return to the bridge for entering harbour. His entry reads: 'Still doing 18 knots but sea now good in vicinity of land.'

As they entered the entrance to Reykjavik, the bridge filled up with sailors in full uniform, including hats, but the guests were still welcome to stare out of the now clear, sea-washed windows. Joanna wrote: 'Suddenly, the Captain demanded silence as he gently manoeuvred Triton into harbour and round a tight corner over to a pier'.

When Reykjavik Television came on board to interview the Hood Association contingent, Joanna said it was most interesting hearing the ex-sailors recount their memories. Den Finden had been in Hood 'most recently', from 1938 - 1940 whereas Ron Paterson and Dick Turner had served in her during the mid-thirties.

After an early lunch with the Captain, Dick retired to make up for lost sleep and prepare for the evening while Joanna and Ron decided to go sightseeing. They had just started when Joanna slipped and fell on the ice, fortunately, without injury. In fact, it was a lucky mishap because it resulted in their being driven round Reykjavik by kind journalist Elin.

They were charmed by some of the City's residential area that featured trim houses each with individually coloured corrugated roofs, window frames and doors. Set against 'the marvellous backdrop of snow-covered mountains' they must have seemed almost unreal. Elin kindly took them to a lovely local building known, most appropriately, as 'The Pearl' because its domed aluminium roof shines at night, like a gleaming jewel.

They were also impressed by a remarkable fountain that spouts the height of the building every few seconds and were treated to coffee and the 'best ever Danish pastries'. The grand finale of their 'conducted tour' was seeing the Hallgrimskirkja (Church), whose steeple they had glimpsed from the ship. When they saw it at close quarters, in all its glory, Joanna said they found it 'absolutely stunning'. The quality of design and craftsmanship inside and out were outstanding and while Ron was naturally impressed by what it stands for as well as its architectural value, both agreed that churches are usually 'examples of the best creations in any area'.

Their last night on board Triton was celebrated with a party given by the Captain in the Officers' Mess. Among the 80 guests were the British Ambassador and his wife, various Naval NATO dignatories several Danish officials and the Commander of the Icelandic Fleet.

As usual, the Galley provided a sumptuous spread and drink flowed as freely as the conversation. Joanna reported that: 'Dick made a speech of thanks and presented the Captain with a Hood Association plaque and the Captain replied with a charming speech and gifts for each of us - a framed print of Triton, a tankard emblazoned with the ship's crest and a badge for a blazer pocket.' She added: 'When the party was just beginning, so no-one could put it down to drink, Lieutenant Commander Jonathan Worthington, representing the Royal Navy, told me that the most moving moment of the Service was when I dropped our fresh flowers. It nearly finished me.'

Dick who was equally affected, wrote: 'When Captain Svend Madsen and I exchanged gifts, he and I embraced like brothers. A long time since I have felt such a sense of kinship. I feel leaving is going to be quite emotional.'

Later in the evening, on behalf of the Association, Joanna extended an invitation to the Captain and his wife to attend the annual Reunion Dinner in May.

Even later, the British group watched themselves on 'Icelandic Telly'.

SUNDAY 16th MARCH

The Captain had kindly invited all his guests to remain until it was time for them for their departure in the afternoon so they all made full use of Triton's extended hospitality.

In Dick's almost completed Log, he wrote: 'Rev. Ron and I were up on the bridge early this morning. Up there and looking out , almost cathedral like. Great peace and serenity.
I am grateful to God and them for making it possible. It will live with me forever'.

In Joanna's first entry for their last day, she noted that when they had 'brunch' at 9.30 a.m., all the men appeared rather the worse for wear as they'd gone to a Reykjavik club in the middle of the night. After consuming vast quantities of orange juice and coffee together with 'revival drinks poured by the Captain', they had a final photograph with as many of the crew as possible and were then piped ashore. And as they drove away, Triton sounded her siren in farewell.

Dick wrote: 'Left ship at 10.50 a.m. We felt, or I feel, that leaving the Captain was like leaving a brother. All the officers and side party were there. Had a minibus tour to the blue lagoon, a hot, out of doors sulphur pool. Needed to keep our bodies well-covered as the outside temperature was freezing,'

Joanna reported that Colin, Rob, Steve and Dick went in for a bracing soak but she, Den and Ron declined. Ron kindly treated them to coffee after she had snapped 'the brave ones being cured of all ills'. They then continued towards the airport, having to dodge lumps of lava edging the road, and went through a decidedly smelly fishing village.

A young Danish sailor drops a single rose in memory of Hood and all those who perished with her.

Dick recorded that: 'After a delay of one and a half hours, flew home. Had a good flight and arrived safely. Thank God'.

The last entry in Joanna's Diary read: 'We have had a quite unforgettable six days. The Danes have been so kind and thoughtful. I have never been so sad to leave a country.

Iceland holds some wonderful memories'.

2001 HOOD EXPEDITION

Now, four years later, another expedition is taking place this summer to help commemorate the 60th anniversary of Hood's loss in a special way.

The official Press Release stated that: 'Respected deep-sea explorer David Mearns, is heading a multi-million pound search for the last resting place of HMS Hood. The search, funded by Channel 4, has the support of the MOD, the Hood Association, the Royal Naval Association and the Royal British Legion. Using state-of-the-art underwater cameras and lighting techniques, the international team aims to locate and film the wreck and establish why she sank so quickly. Updates of the search will be available round the world via a constantly updated internet site. There will also be live programmes and a full-length documentary later in the year.'

In his statement, Expedition Co-ordinator Rob White of ITN said: 'Our plans are simply to find the wreck, film it with sensitivity and respect and at the long term request of the HMS Hood Association, place a memorial plaque at the site. We will be accompanied by leading Naval historians'

President of the Hood Association Ted Briggs, the sole living survivor, added his full approval for the expedition: 'I am very happy that 60 years on, the great sacrifice of my friends and shipmates in the Mighty Hood is being so fully recognised'.

The Expedition's Finale
July 2001

Ted Briggs' farewell to his many former shipmates was a fitting finale to a remarkable expedition that succeeded in both locating Hood's grave and filming some of the most moving pictures of a wreck ever seen on our screens.

Experts were surprised by the extent of the damage to the once Mighty Hood and the fact that the largest portion of the hull was upside down. But some of the amazing images show the still

210

discernible bows and a few poignant relics such as the ship's bell, some anti-aircraft ammunition and the flag staff still in place on her stern.

Part of the affecting climax to Hood's discovery was the lowering of the memorial plaque. Constructed of solid brass, it has a central disc digitally engraved with the names of all who perished with her and is designed to withstand the weight of water, perhaps for centuries.

Finally, at the end of a short Service, Ted cast a wreath into the sea and said the ever-moving words of remembrance.........

> *"They shall grow not old, as we that are left grow old. Age shall not weary them, nor the years condemn. At the going down of the sun and in the morning. We will remember them."*

CHAPTER NINE

While the main part of this book 'centres on the lives and memories of those still with us' who served in HMS Hood and continue to cherish the experience.this final section is dedicated to the memory of those who perished with her, sixty years ago.

It contains the Roll of Honour listing the names of all 1,418 men who lost their lives and some of the Memorial Gallery photographs available in time for inclusion. It is hoped that a more extensive 'Gallery' will be published at a later date, accompanied by all existing biographical records.

ROLL OF HONOUR

A

Abbott, Frederick	Marine	RM
Abbott, Kenneth	Ordinary Coder	RN
Ablett, Wallace A	Marine	RM
Abrams, Robert G	Cook	RN
Acton, Percival C H	Able Seaman	RN
Adams, Frank	Musician	RM
Adams, Keith H	Corporal	RM
Adams, Nigel N	Midshipman	RN
Adams, Victor E	Ordinary Seaman	RN
Adams, Victor H	Leading Stoker	RN
Ainsworth, Fred. J	Able Seaman	RN
Akehurst, Rodney G	Stoker First Class	RN

Aldred, Gerald A	Ordinary Telephonist	RN
Algate, Alfred K	Canteen Assistant	NAAFI
Alger, Eric	Ordinary Seaman	RN
Alland, Harry C	Petty Officer	RN
Alcock, William S	Boy 1st Class	RN
Allen, Arthur	Leading Stoker	RN
Allen, Charles	Leading Seaman	RN
Allen, Edward B	Ordinary Seaman	RN
Allen, James E	Stoker 1st Class	RN
Allen, John G	Marine	RM
Allen, William E S	Able Seaman	RN
Allott, George	Marine	RM
Almond, Frederick	Able Seaman	RN
Altham, Arthur	Stoker 2nd Class	RN
Ambridge, Walter	Sergeant	RM
Ambrose, John	Able Seaman	RN
Amery, Thomas C F	Able Seaman	RN
Anderson, Arthur D	Ordinary Seaman	RN
Anderson, John	Chief Engine Room Artificer	RN
Anderson, Joseph M	Ordinary Seaman	RN
Andrews, Cecil V	Ordinary Seaman	RN
Annis, James E	Stoker 1st Class	RN
Applegarth, Richard	Leading Signalman	RN
Appleyard, John A F	Ordinary Seaman	RN
Ardly, Jack C	Boy 1st Class	RN
Arkinstall, John	Leading Seaman	RN
Armstrong, John C	Leading Stocker	RN
Armstrong, Norman	Able Seaman	RN
Arnold, William A	Stoker Petty Officer	RN
Ashley, Robert G	Able Seaman	RN
Assirati, Albert F	Stoker Petty Officer	RN
Aston, John	Electrical Artificer 4th Class	RN
Atkins, William E	Chief Petty Officer Steward	RN
Atkinson, John H	Able Seaman	RN
Atkinson, Robert	Stoker Petty Officer	RN
Austin, Albert G L	Able Seaman	RN
Avery, Albert G	Able Seaman	RN
Awdry, C D	Lieutenant-Commander	RN
Ayling, Frank R	Canteen Assistant	NAAFI
Ayling, Ronald	Able Seaman	RN
Ayres, Henry D	Ordinary Signalman	RN

B

Badcock, John H	Stoker 1st Class	RN
Bailton, Frank	Able Seaman	RN
Bailey, Frederick W	Marine	RM
Bailey, Leonard W J	Ordinary Signalman	RN
Baines, Godfrey J	Leading Seaman	RN
Baker, Andrew L	Ordinary Seaman	RN
Baker, George E	Leading Stoker	RN
Baker, Kenneth A	Petty Officer Telegraphist	RN
Balch, Percy H	Able Seaman	RN
Baldwin, Kenneth E G	Stoker 1st Class	RN
Baldwin, Phillip R	Ordinary Seaman	RN
Ball, Charles F D	Able Seaman	RN
Ball, Phillip A	Stoker 1st Class	RN
Ball, William	Leading Stoker	RN
Ballard, Arthur	Boy 1st Class	RN
Balsdon, Ernest F	Stoker 1st Class	RN
Balston, Kenneth	Signal Boy	RN
Bamford, Antony J	Able Seaman	RN
Banfield, Kenneth J	Boy 1st Class	RN
Banks, George H	Stoker 1st Class	RN
Banks, Sidney T	Leading Cook (S)	RN
Barclay, Alex T	Leading Cook (S)	RN
Barker, Thomas	Ordinary Seaman	RN
Barnes, Thomas G	Petty Officer Stoker	RN
Barnes, Walter J	Able Seaman	RN
Barnet, William L	Cook (O)	RN
Barnett, Ivor G	Stoker 2nd Class	RN
Barrie, Walter R	Able Seaman	RN
Barringer, William H	Marine	RM
Bartley, Archibald E T	Signal Boatswain	RN
Barton, Kenneth C F	Petty Officer	RN
Basham, Howard	Ordinary Seaman	RN
Bassett, Charles G	Petty Officer	RN
Basstone, Jack	Marine	RM
Batchelor, Arthur R	Yeoman of Signals	RN
Bates, Frederick G	Leading Seaman	RN
Bates, Leonard A	Marine	RM
Bates, Reginald S	Wireman	RN
Batley, Anthony R T	Lieutenant-Commander	RNVR

Batten, Herbert W L	Ordinary Seaman	RN
Battersby, Clifford	Able Seaman	RN
Baxter, John K	Petty Officer	RN
Bayliss, Herbert J	Ordinary Signalman	RN
Beard, Alan	Marine	RM
Beard, Thomas N K	Midshipman	RCN
Beardsley, Geoffrey V	Joiner 4th Class	RN
Belcher, Cyril S V	Electrical Artificer 3rd Class	RN
Bell, Cyril K	Ordinary Signalman	RN
Bell, Ronald T L	Ordinary Signalman	RN
Bell, William	Able Seaman	RN
Belsham, James R	Able Seaman	RN
Bembridge, Percy A	Ordinary Seaman	RN
Bennett, Ernest	Marine	RM
Bennett, Percival	Boy 1st Class	RN
Benoist, Donald G	Able Seaman	RN
Benwell, Ernest F T	Sick Berth Chief Petty Officer	RN
Berner, Robert V	Leading Writer	RN
Betts, Robert	Stoker 1st Class	RN
Beveridge, Roy	Ordnance Artificer 4th Class	RN
Biggenden, Walden J	Chief Stoker	RN
Binnie, John E	Petty Officer Stoker	RN
Bird, Herbert G A	Ordnance Artificer 3rd Class	RN
Bishop, Charles J	Chief Stoker	RN
Bishop, Edward J P	Petty Officer	RN
Bispham, Leslie W	Ordinary Seaman	RN
Biss, John	Able Seaman	RN
Blake, Harold G	Leading Stoker	RN
Blann, Kenneth A F	Able Seaman	RN
Bleach, Arthur B	Able Seaman	RN
Bloodworth, Herbert W	Able Seaman	RN
Blow, Leonard	Ordinary Seaman	RN
Blunt, William H T	Leading Cook (S)	RN
Blurton, Reginald	Ordinary Seaman	RN
Boardman, Stanley	Petty Officer	RN
Bocutt, Alfred A	Marine	RM
Boncey, William L	Petty Officer	RN
Bond, Sidney W	Able Seaman	RN
Boneham, Norman	Marine	RM
Boniface, Jack	Able Seaman	RN
Bonner, Colin A	Able Seaman	RN

Boone, Bernard J	Engine Room Artificer 4th Class	RN
Booth, George H	Stoker 2nd Class	RN
Borrer, Harold T	Able Seaman	RN
Borsberry, George	Petty Officer Cook (S)	RN
Bosley, Frank W	Leading Sick Berth Attendant	RN
Bostock, Charles W	Chief Mechanician	RN
Bower, Reginald P	Able Seaman	RN
Bower, Ronald	Stoker 1st Class	RN
Bowers, Leo S	Ordinary Seaman	RN
Bowie, Duncan	Able Seaman	RN
Bowyer, Thomas R	Ordinary Telegraphist	RN
Bowyer, Walter F	Stoker 1st Class	RN
Bradley, Harold	Ordinary Seaman	RN
Bradley, Kenneth J	Able Seaman	RN
Bradshaw, Thomas F	Stoker 2nd Class	RN
Bramhall, Harold	Joiner 4th Class	RN
Brand, William H	Corporal	RM
Brandon, Albert A	Ordinary Telegraphist	RN
Bransden, Paul D	Able Seaman	RN
Brett, Benjamin A	Ordinary Seaman	RN
Brewer, Arthur W	Ordinary Seaman	RN
Brewer, George	Ordinary Seaman	RN
Bridge, Arthur T	Telegraphist	RN
Bridges, Kenneth C	Ordinary Telegraphist	RN
Bridges, Ronald W	Wireman	RN
Brierley, William L	Leading Steward	RN
Bristow, Harry	Wireman	RN
Britton, Clarence V	Marine	RM
Broadhurst, Dennis C	Wireman	RN
Broadley, William	Leading Seaman	RN
Brookes, Donald A	Telegraphist	RN
Brooks, Gordon B	Stoker 1st Class	RN
Brooks, Jack	Stoker 1st Class	RN
Brooks, Terrence L	Marine	RM
Broom, George W	Shipwright 3rd Class	RN
Brown, Arthur	Marine	RM
Brown, Eric	Boy 1st Class	RN
Brown, Ernest	Stoker 2nd Class	RN
Brown, George	Steward	RN
Brown, Henry J	Able Seaman	RN
Brown, John L	Leading Seaman	RN

Brown, Robert K	Petty Officer Stoker	RN
Browne. Robert P	Lieutenant (S)	RN
Brownrigg, John G P	Lieutenant-Commander	RN
Bryant, Denis M	Midshipman	RN
Buck, Arthur E J	Mechanician 2nd Class	RN
Buck, Herbert T J	Petty Officer Stoker	RN
Buckett, Philip J	Midshipman	RNVR
Bull, Percival H	Leading Seaman	RN
Bull, Robert J	Able Seaman	RN
Bullock, Edward H	Able Seaman	RN
Bullock, Henry W	Marine	RN
Bullock, William	Able Seaman	RN
Bulman, Kenneth F	Petty Officer	RN
Burckitt, John B E	Petty Officer Cook	RN
Burgess, Henry	Warrant Ordnance Officer	RN
Burkin, Robert H	Marine	RM
Burnell, Gordon R	Ordinary Seaman	RN
Burningham, William F W R		
	Chief Petty Officer	RN
Burns, Albert S	Able Seaman	RN
Bussey, Harry F	Able Seaman	RN
Butlar, Horace A	Able Seaman	RN
Butterworth, Alfred N	Able Seaman	RN
Byrne, Francis	Boy 1st Class	RN
Byrne, Thomas G	Stoker 1st Class	RN

C

Cabell, Percy A	Chief Petty Officer Cook	RN
Cabrin, Roy V	Stoker 2nd Class	RN
Callon, William J	Boy 1st Class	RN
Cambridge, John H	Sub-Lieutenant (E)	RNVR
Campbell, Albert G	Leading Seaman	RN
Cann, Herbert R	Marine	RM
Cantrill, Joshua	Petty Officer Stoker	RN
Canty, William D	Yeoman of Signals	RN
Capon, Leslie A	Ordinary Seaman	RN
Capstick, Arthur J	Marine	RM
Carey, Arthur T	Ordinary Seaman	RN
Carey, Daniel A B	Supply Assistant	RN
Carlin, George V	Lieutenant-Commander	RNVR

Cam, George H K	Chief Yeoman of Signals	RN
Carpenter, Robert S	Marine	RM
Carr, John	Stoker 2nd Class	RN
Carter, Robert J W	Marine	RM
Cartwright, Thomas D	Captain	RM
Cavell, Percy H	Stoker 1st Class	RN
Chamberlain, Henry S	Corporal	RM
Chandler, Arthur J	Master at Arms	RN
Chaplin, Albert E	Boy 1st Class	RN
Chapman, James A	Commissioned Gunner	RN
Chappell, Robert E	Able Seaman	RN
Charker, Albert W	Able Seaman	RN
Charlton, Robert A	Able Seaman	RN
Chatfield, Edwin H	Able Seaman	RN
Cheadle, Henry J	Petty Officer	RN
Chivers, William A	Engine Room Artificer 3rd Class	RN
Choules, Sydney J	Chief Petty Officer	RN
Chowney, William H	Chief Petty Officer	RN
Churchill, Ronald J	Ordinary Seaman	RN
Claringbold, Leon J	Able Seaman	RN
Clark, Jack C P	Ordinary Seaman	RN
Clark, John French	Leading Seaman	RN
Clark, Robert G	Marine	RM
Clarke, David W	Ordinary Seaman	RN
Clarke, Leslie H	Electrical Artificer 4th Class	RN
Clarke, Stanley W	Wireman	RN
Clayton, Stanley	Wireman	RN
Clayton, William A	Ordinary Seaman	RN
Cleeter, William G	Able Seaman	RN
Clements, Thomas W	Able Seaman	RN
Cleton, Peter V	Engine Room Artificer 4th Class	RN
Clitherow, Charles F	Stoker 2nd Class	RN
Clothier, Kenneth R J	Ordinary Coder	RN
Clout, Cecil G	Able Seaman	RN
Cobb, William H	Ordinary Seaman	RN
Cockhead, Alfred J	Leading Stoker	RN
Cogger, Thomas E	Marine	RM
Cole, Albert E	Ordinary Seaman	RN
Cole, George D	Marine	RM
Cole, John H	Able Seaman	RN
Cole, William G	Marine	RM

Colemen, Dennis J	Marine	RM
Collett, Stanley J	Able Seaman	RN
Collings, John P	Midshipman (S)	RN
Collins, Arthur R	Petty Officer	RN
Collins, Reginald J	Able Seaman	RN
Collinson, Robert	Boy 1st Class	RN
Collis, Gordon V	Boy 1st Class	RN
Collyer, Percy W L	Boy 1st Class	RN
Comber James D	Leading Seaman	RN
Coombes, Richard A L	Ordinary Seaman	RN
Compton, William A	Leading Stoker	RN
Conchie, William M	Boy 1st Class	RN
Conroy, Cornelius	Stoker 2nd Class	RN
Constable, Alan R	Boy 1st Class	RN
Cook, James E	Chief Stoker	RN
Cook, Joseph R	Able Seaman	RN
Cook, Vernon	Blacksmith 4th Class	RN
Coombes, Gerald E	Sergeant	RM
Cooper, Alan C	Able Seaman	RN
Cooper, Frederick G D	Mechanician 2nd Class	RN
Cooper, Geoffrey G	Able Seaman	RN
Cooper, George W	Ordinary Coder	RN
Cooper, John	Marine	RM
Cope, George R	Boy 1st Class	RN
Cope, Sidney J	Commissioned Gunner	RN
Corddell, Harold L	Chief Petty Officer	RN
Corlett, John	Engine Room Artificer 4th Class	RN
Cornock, James	Able Seaman	RN
Cotton, Lewis A	Stoker 2nd Class	RN
Cottrell, Albert E	Ordinary Seaman	RN
Coulson, John	Musician	RM
Coulthurst, Francis B	Stoker 2nd Class	RN
Court, William R	Able Seaman	RN
Cowie, John E L	Shipwright 4th Class	RN
Cox, Arthur J	Ordinary Seaman	RN
Cox, Cyril A	Stoker 1st Class	RN
Cox, John F	Wireman	RN
Cox, Leslie L	Ordinary Coder	RN
Cox, Stanley K	Leading Seaman	RN
Craft, Thomas E	Able Seaman	RN
Cranston, Aylmer N J	Stoker 1st Class	RN

Crawford, William M	Boy 1st Class	RN
Crawley, Lawrence	Stoker 1st Class	RN
Crawte, Alfred E J	Musician	RM
Crellin, William	Stoker 1st Class	RN
Cresswell, Henry R	Marine	RM
Cross, Joseph B	Petty Officer	RN
Cross, Robert C	Cook (O)	RN
Cross, William K R	Commander	RN
Crouch, Cecil H	Petty Officer Regulating	RN
Croucher, Lambert E	Able Seaman	RN
Crow, George L	Leading Stoker	RN
Crumpton, Lawrence	Leading Stoker	RN
Cruttenden, John E	Able Seaman	RN
Cunningham, John	Able Seaman	RN
Cunningham, Richard F	Ordinary Seaman	RN
Currie, George	Stoker 1st Class	RN
Currie, Robert	Stoker 1st Class	RN
Cuthbert, Albert T	Corporal	RM
Czeruy, S	Midshipman	PN

D

D'Abry De L'Arves, Robert		
	Able Seaman	RN
Dade, William F L	Petty Officer Steward	RN
Dakers, William B	Sick Berth Attendant	RN
Dale, Richard E	Lieutenant (E)	RN
Dall,Francis O	Able Seaman	RN
Dalziel, Thomas	Ordinary Signalman	RN
Daniels, Charles G	Stoker 1st Class	RN
Darby, Leonard	Ordinary Seaman	RN
Davey, Frederick G	Leading Telegraphist	RN
Davey, Reginald J	Able Seaman	RN
Davies, Douglas A	Able Seaman	RN
Davies, Frederick M	Able Seaman	RN
Davies, Hamilton K	Midshipman	RNVR
Davies, Horace D	Lieutenant	RM
Davies, Kenneth James	Boy Bugler	RM
Davies, Ronald T	Sen. Master Commis. Warrant Officer	
		RN
Davis, Gordon E	Able Seaman	RN

Davis, Herbert A	Marine	RM
Davis, Percy J	Stoker 1st Class	RN
Dawson, Phillip J	Signal Boy	RN
Day, Frederick J	Marine	RM
Day, William S W	Chief Electrical Artificer	RN
De Gernier, James B	Able Seaman	RNVR
De St George, Edward O	Able Seaman	RN
De Ste Croix, Cyril R	Leading Stoker	RN
Dean, Cyril A J	Stoker 1st Class	RN
Dean, George A	Signalman	RN
Dear, Nelson L	Musician	RM
Dempsey, Martin	Able Seaman	RN
Denault, Benjamin	Stoker 2nd Class	RN
Dennis, Ronald	Able Seaman	RN
Dent, Christopher H C	Surgeon Lieutenant	RNVR
Derrick, Charles T	Leading Supply Assistant	RN
Devereaux, Albert	Ordinary Seaman	RN
Dewey, Edward D G	Boy 1st Class	RN
Diggens, James B	Able Seaman	RN
Dilly, John H C	Stoker 1st Class	RN
Dinsdale, Stanley	Stoker 1st Class	RN
Discombe, Archie	Musician	RM
Ditchburn, Edward	Ordinary Signalman	RN
Dixon, Albert	Leading Stoker	RN
Dixon, William	Able Seaman	RN
Doak, Walter W	Petty Officer	RN
Dobeson, Nicholas	Chief Petty Officer	RN
Dobson, Charles W	Able Seaman	RN
Dockrill, Harold	Able Seaman	RN
Dodd, Henry	Stoker 1st Class	RN
Donaghy, Walter	Able Seaman	RN
Donald, James H	Boy 1st Class	RN
Donaldson, Walter M H	Ordinary Seaman	RN
Doolan, Francis	Stoker 2nd Class	RN
Douglas, Neil H	Able Seaman	RN
Douglass, Mark R	Boy 1st Class	RN
Dowdles, Malcolm M	Able Seaman	RNVR
Dowdell, William F	Leading Seaman	RN
Down, John R	Sub-Lieutenant	RNVR
Druken, Valentine	Ordinary Seaman	RN
Drury, Ernest	Ordinary Signalman	RN

Duckworth, Kenneth R R	Able Seaman	RN
Dudman, Caleb A W	Mechanician 1st Class	RN
Duffiels, John	Stoker 1st Class	RN
Dunn, Stephen E	Able Seaman	RN
Dunne, Patrick L	Petty Officer	RN
Dunnell, Graham G	Marine	RM
Dunwell, William S	Able Seaman	RN
Dyas, Richard J	Stoker 2nd Class	RN
Dyment, Herbert R	Ordinary Seaman	RN

E

Eagles, George R	Midshipman	RN
Earl, Joseph W	Stoker 2nd Class	RN
Earwaker, Ronald C	Able Seaman	RN
Eastwood, Walter C	Marine	RM
Eaton, Raymond K J	Leading Stoker	RN
Eaves, Leonard	Wireman	RN
Edes, Henry M	Able Seaman	RN
Edminson, Reginald F	Chief Engine Room Artificer	RN
Edmonds, Alfred G	Able Seaman	RN
Edmonds, Anthony R	Writer	RN
Edwards, Melville	Marine	RM
Edwards, Robert	Stoker 2nd Class	RN
Edwards, Thomas W G	Able Seaman	RN
Eldred, Eric C	Stoker 1st Class	RN
Eldridge, Bertie D M	Stoker 2nd Class	RN
Elliott, John G	Petty Officer Stoker	RN
Eltis, Donald O	Ordinary Seaman	RN
Emery, Lawrence A	Musician	RM
Emery, Richard C	Petty Officer Stoker	RN
Erridge, Frank A	Telegraphist	RN
Erskine, John G M	Lieutenant-Commander (E)	RN
Erskine, Roy D	Signalman	RN
Escott, Robert W	Stoker 2nd Class	RN
Evans, David m	Stoker 2nd Class	RN
Ewart-James, David E	Ordinary Seaman	RN
Eyres, Thomas W W	Able Seaman	RN

F

Fair, George W	Shipwright 4th Class	RN

Fairlie, Percy W	Stoker 1st Class	RN
Farmer, Albert V	Leading Seaman	RN
Farnish, Frederick N	Petty Officer Telegraphist	RN
Farrar, Clifton	Marine	RM
Faulkner, Ronald E	Stoker 1st Class	RN
Fenner, Henry J	Marine	RM
Field, Edgar C	Ordinary Signalman	RN
Fielder, Jack H	Able Seaman	RN
Fielding, James O	Surgeon Lieutenant	RN
Finch, John L	Boy 1st Class	RN
Finlayson, David A	Able Seaman	RNVR
Fisher, Leslie	Blacksmith 3rd Class	RN
Fitch, Edward G	Able Seaman	RN
Fitchew, Cecil A	Ordinary Seaman	RN
Fitzgerald, Joseph V	Ordinary Seaman	RN
Fletcher, Peter	Petty Officer Stoker	RN
Fletcher, Victor W J	Able Seaman	RN
Flint, Sydney G	Able Seaman	RN
Floyd, Charles	Wireman	RN
Flynn, John T	Stoker 2nd Class	RN
Foden, Leslie J	Leading Seaman	RN
Foley, Rodney A	Chief Stoker	RN
Foot, Charles	Leading Stoker	RN
Ford, Douglas C	Midshipman	RNR
Ford, Harold E	Ordinary Seaman	RN
Ford, Jack	Able Seaman	RN
Forrest, Ernest W	Writer	RN
Forrest, George M D	Wireman	RN
Forrest, Victor	Petty Officer Steward	RN
Forrester, John J	Chief Petty Officer Writer	RN
Forster, Frederick G	Engine Room Artificer 4th Class	RN
Foster, Algernon T	Able Seaman	RN
Foster, Colin E	Ordinary Seaman	RN
Foster, Kenneth J	Able Seaman	RN
Foster, Ralph	Ordinary Seaman	RN
Foster, Reginald	Able Seaman	RN
Fotheringham, George	Marine	RM
Fowle, Henry J	Able Seaman	RN
Fowler, Frank S	Ordinary Signalman	RN
Fowler, Robert H	Musician	RM
Francis, Charles A	Boy 1st Class	RN

Francis, Victor R	Leading Stoker	RN
Freeborn, Frederick C	Warrant Supply Officer	RN
Freeman, Douglas E	Ordinary Seaman	RN
Freeman, Mark H P	Midshipman	RNR
French, Leslie V	Ordinary Seaman	RN
French, Ronald M	Ordnance Artificer 4th Class	RN
Friend, Leslie E	Lieutenant	RNVR
Frodsham, Neville H	Acting Sub-Lieutenant	RN
Fry, John C	Ordinary Coder	RN
Fullick, Frederick R	Able Seaman	RN
Funnell, Kevin G	Ordinary Seaman	RN

G

Gabbett, Cecil P	Ordinary Seaman	RN
Gale, Ronald M	Stoker 1st Class	RN
Gallacher, Cornwall	Ordinary Signalman	RN
Gallant, Joseph	Ordinary Seaman	RN
Gallant, William	Ordinary Seaman	RN
Galliott, Howard W	Ordinary Seaman	RN
Galloway, Arthur	Engine Room Artificer 4th Class	RN
Gardner, James D	Petty Officer Telegraphist	RN
Garman, Victor G	Leading Stoker	RN
Garroway, Robert L	Steward	RN
Garry, Neville W H	Ordinary Telegraphist	RN
Gasgoine, Thomas K	Able Seaman	RN
Gaudet, Samuel	Ordinary Seaman	RN
Genaway, Victor W	Ordinary Seaman	RN
Gibb, Stanley D	Wireman	RN
Gibbon, Isaac G	Chief Ordnance Artificer	RN
Gibbs, Charles W E	Leading Signalman	RN
Gibson, James	Stoker 2nd Class	RN
Gibson, John H	Signalman	RN
Gibson, Thomas	Marine	RM
Giffen, John A	Stoker 2nd Class	RN
Gilbert, Charles E G	Stoker 1st Class	RN
Gilbert, Harold	Able Seaman	RN
Gillan, Joseph	Marine	RM
Gillett, George P	Ordinary Seaman	RN
Gillis, John R	Ordinary Seaman	RN
Glass, Leslie G V	Able Seaman	RN

Gledhill, James E	Corporal	RM
Glenn, Robert	Petty Officer Stoker	RN
Goddard, Sidney	Able Seaman	RN
Goff, Jack	Boy 1st Class	RN
Goldsmith, Horace W	Petty Officer	RN
Gomer, Harry	Marine	RM
Gomershall, Royston	Ordinary Seaman	RN
Good, Bernard E C	Marine	RM
Good, Frederick A	Petty Officer	RN
Goodbody, John W	Stoker 1st Class	RN
Goodenough, Herbert H	Cook (S)	RN
Gordon, Leslie S	Able Seaman	RN
Gough, John M	Colour Sergeant	RM
Goulstine, Leonard	Able Seaman	RN
Graham, Donald	Supply Assistant	RN
Graves, John R	Lieutenant (S)	RNVR
Gray, Alfred E E	Able Seaman	RN
Gray, John C	Ordinary Seaman	RN
Green, Benjamin L	Marine	RM
Green, Harry	Able Seaman	RN
Green, Herbert	Signal Boy	RN
Green, John H	Ordinary Signalman	RN
Green, William J	Leading Stoker	RN
Green, William J	Ordinary Signalman	RN
Greene, Derek A	Ordinary Signalman	RN
Gregory, Arthur H	Leading Seaman	RN
Gregory, John	Marine	RM
Gregson, Edward H G	Commander	RN
Griffin, Charles A	Marine	RM
Griffiths, Leonard F	Ordinary Seaman	RN
Grogan, Robert T	Commander (E)	RN
Groucott, Roland D	Able Seaman	RN
Groves, Stedman B	Musician	RM
Groves, Thomas	Able Seaman	RN
Grundy, Frederick E	Wireman	RN
Guest, Alan	Band Boy	RM
Gulliver, Edward G V	Leading Seaman	RN

H

Haden-Morris, Alec B	Supply Assistant	RN

Hadley, Alan E	Ordinary Seaman	RN
Hadow, Norman W A	Ordinary Seaman	RN
Haeger, Edward G	Sergeant	RM
Hales, Edward	Able Seaman	RN
Hall, David G	Ordinary Seaman	RN
Hall, George W	Ordinary Seaman	RN
Hall, Henry G	Able Seaman	RN
Hall, John W	Lieutenant-Commander	RN
Hall, Neville T	Signalman	RN
Hall, Norman V	Stoker 1st Class	RN
Hall, Thomas	Marine	RM
Halls, Wilfred C	Ordinary Signalman	RN
Hambley, Thomas H	Able Seaman	RN
Hanna, Robert	Plumber 3rd Class	RN
Hannaway, Edward J	Ordinary Telegraphist	RN
Hannay, James D	Stoker 2nd Class	RN
Hanwell, Tom	Chief Stoker	RN
Harding, John S	Able Seaman	RN
Harding, William	Stoker 1st Class	RN
Hardy, Henry FM	Cook (S)	RN
Harkess, Robert W	Stoker 1st Class	RN
Harkison, Thomas	Able Seaman	RN
Harler, Douglas B	Able Seaman	RN
Harmer, George	Engine Room Artificer 4th Class	RN
Harris, Charles A	Chief Mechanician	RN
Harris, Desmond S R	Lieutenant	RM
Harris, Frank R	Ordnance Artificer 4th Class	RN
Harris, James A	Marine	RM
Hartly, Arthur	Boy 1st Class	RN
Hartley, Norman	Stoker 2nd Class	RN
Hartmann, Geoffrey H	Ordinary Coder	RN
Harty, Jack	Leading Seaman	RN
Harvey, Edward R	Leading Cook (O)	RN
Harvey, Eric O	Stoker 2nd Class	RN
Hastings, Joseph	Able Seaman	RN
Hatherill, William H	Marine	RM
Haughton, Cyril	Warrant Engineer	RN
Hawkey, Derrick B	Signalman	RN
Hawkins, Ernest H	Shipwright 1st Class	RN
Hawthorne, Arthur W	Wireman	RN
Hawthorne, John W	Petty Officer Cook (O)	RN

Hayde, Joseph	Leading Seaman	RN
Haynes, Albert E	Leading Stoker	RN
Hayton, John W	Able Seaman	RN
Heath, David J	Ordinary Seaman	RN
Heaton, Albert	Able Seaman	RN
Hellens, Joseph S	Engine Room Artificer 4th Class	RN
Hemmings, Bertie	Engine Room Artificer 4th Class	RN
Henderson, John	Signalman	RN
Hendry, William	Marine	RM
Heneway, Victor W	Boy 1st Class	RN
Hennessy, David T	Boy 1st Class	RN
Henshaw, Owen W	Stoker 1st Class	RN
Henshaw, Ronald	Boy 1st Class	RN
Heptonstall, George A	Able Seaman	RN
Herbert, Sidney J	Captain (E)	RN
Hermon, Eric D	Marine	RM
Herod, Maurice H E	Bandmaster	RM
Heys, William W	Sick Berth Attendant	RN
Hibbs, Francis H F	Corporal	RM
Hibbs, Richard A	Midshipman	RNVR
Hickman, Leonard A	Stoker 2nd Class	RN
Hickmott, William J	Boy 1st Class	RN
Higgins, Michael	Ordinary Seaman	RN
Higginson, William	Stoker 1st Class	RN
Higgott, John N	Engine Room Artificer 3rd Class	RN
Hill, Eric J R	Marine	RM
Hilton, Albert F	Stoker 1st Class	RN
Hiscock, Frederick J	Marine	RM
Hiscock, William A	Petty Officer	RN
Hives, Ronald	Stoker 1st Class	RN
Hoare, Cyril A	Stoker 2nd Class	RN
Hoare, Norris H	Lieutenant (S)	RNVR
Hobbs, Frederick J	Chief Stoker	RN
Hobbs, Robert	Engine Room Artificer 4th Class	RN
Hogan, John M	Commander (S)	RN
Holdaway, Frank	Joiner 1st Class	RN
Holland, Charles	Marine	RM
Holland, Francis H	Stoker 1st Class	RN
Holland, Lancelot E	Vice-Admiral	RN
Hollis, Bramwell G	Ordinary Signalman	RN
Holmes, Edward J	Boy 1st Class	RN

Holmes, George	Leading Stoker	RN
Holmes, Harold	Able Seaman	RN
Holroyd, Arthur	Sailmaker's Mate	RN
Homer, Harold	Chief Mechanician	RN
Honeybun, Richard J	Chief Stoker	RN
Hoole, Horace	Leading Stoker	RN
Hope, Ernest J	Leading Stoker	RN
Horner, Leslie	Able Seaman	RN
Horsman, Lawrence	Leading Cook (S)	RN
Horton, George W	Petty Officer Steward	RN
Howard, Eric S	Ordinary Seaman	RN
Howe, Reginald E	Stoker 2nd Class	RN
Howie, Robert G W	Marine	RM
Howlett, Patrick	Ordinary Seaman	RN
Hows, Gordon	Marine	RM
Howse, Thomas	Leading Seaman	RN
Hoyle, Sidney	Ordinary Seaman	RN
Hughes, Hugh	Leading Stoker	RN
Hughes, William F	Marine	RM
Hull, Arthur W	Able Seaman	RN
Hulme, Arthur	Wireman	RN
Hulme, Owen E	Able Seaman	RN
Humphrey, Michael ST	Lieutenant (E)	RN
Humphreys, William	Marine	RM
Hunns, John A C	Marine	RM
Hunt, George	Stoker 2nd Class	RN
Hunt, William N	Ordnance Artificer 1st Class	RN
Hunter, John M J	Ordinary Seaman	RN
Huntington, Ernest S	Sergeant	RM
Huntley, Henry F	Plumber 1st Class	RN
Hurle, Ronald C	Supply Assistant	RN
Hurst, Christopher W	Coder	RN
Hurst, Henry	Commander-Surgeon	RN
Huskinson, Sydney	Able Seaman	RN
Hutchings, Leslie W R	Painter 3rd Class	RN
Hutchins, Albert J	Petty Officer	RN

I

Iago, John M	Electrical Lieutenant	RN
Ierston, Kenneth W	Ordinary Seaman	RN

Ingram, John W	Able Seaman	RN
Ingram, Leslie R	Able Seaman	RN
Inkpen, Reginald S	Stoker 1st Class	RN
Innes, Alexander	Able Seaman	RN

J

Jack, George	Ordinary Seaman	RN
Jackson, George S	Marine	RM
Jaggers, Eric	Stoker 2nd Class	RN
James, Leonard A	Leading Stoker	RN
James, Phillip A	Ordinary Seaman	RN
Jarvis, Arthur C	Able Seaman	RN
Jarvis, Leonard R	Able Seaman	RN
Javan, Kenneth W	Ordinary Seaman	RN
Jeffs, Norman	Stoker 1st Class	RN
Jelley, Stanley A	Boy 1st Class	RN
Jennings, Walter H W	Chief Petty Officer	RN
Jesse, Harold	Chief Electrical Artificer	RN
John, Thomas	Marine	RM
Johnson, Frederick	Leading Cook	RN
Johnson, Ralph	Stoker 1st Class	RN
Johnson, Stanley F	Leading Writer	RN
Johnson, William F	Petty Officer	RN
Johnson, William S C	Petty Officer Stoker	RN
Johnston, James	Able Seaman	RN
Johnston, William	Assistant Steward	RN
Johnstone, Norman	Signal Boy	RN
Jones, Albert J	Able Seaman	RN
Jones, David J	Leading Stoker	RN
Jones, Francis L L	Midshipman	RCN
Jones, Frederick R	Able Seaman	RN
Jones, Gordon H	Stoker 1st Class	RN
Jones, Gwilym	Able Seaman	RN
Jones, Harold H	Able Seaman	RN
Jones, Hayden J	Stoker 1st Class	RN
Jones, James W	Petty Officer Stoker	RN
Jones, John W	Petty Officer	RN
Jones, Kenneth	Ordinary Seaman	RN
Jones, Richard	Seaman	RNR
Jones, Robert	Boy 1st Class	RN

Jones, Ronald G S	Ordinary Seaman	RN
Jones, Roy T R	Boy 1st Class	RN
Jordan, Geoffrey W	Canteen Assistant	NAAFI
Jordan, Kenneth F A	Leading Cook (S)	RN
Joyce, Leslie R	Boy 1st Class	RN
Julier, Alfred E	Marin	RM

K

Kay, Norman	Engine Room Artificer 3rd Class	RN
Kay, Samuel	Ordinary Seaman	RN
Keal, George F	Leading Stoker	RN
Kean, Albert A	Petty Officer Telegraphist	RN
Kearney, Thomas P	Seaman	RNR
Keating, Kenneth H W	Able Seaman	RN
Keenan, Robert J	Stoker 1st Class	RN
Keens, Eric G	Boy Telegraphist	RN
Keers, Robert	Boy 1st Class	RN
Keith, Arthur W	Marine	RM
Kelly, Cornelius	Ordinary Signalman	RN
Kelly, Jack V K	Able Seaman	RN
Kelly, John	Ordnance Artificer 4th Class	RN
Kelly, Robert	Petty Officer Stoker	RN
Kemish, Colin H T	Boy 1st Class	RN
Kempton, Sylvius L	Ordinary Signalman	RN
Kendall, Albert J	Able Seaman	RN
Kerr, Alexander	Engine Room Artificer	RN
Kerr, Ralph	Captain HMS Hood	RN
Kerr, Raymond W	Boy 1st Class	RN
Kerridge, Herbert	Stoker 1st Class	RN
Kersley, Albert S	Marine	RM
King, Ernest H	Able Seaman	RN
King, Howard L C	Signalman	RNVR
King, William A	Able Seaman	RN
Kingston, Jack	Able Seaman	RN
Kinmond, Charles H	Able Seaman	RN
Kirk, Alfred	Ordinary Telegraphist	RN
Kirk, Russell G	Marine	RM
Kirkland, John D	Able Seaman	RN
Kitchener, Reginald J	Able Seaman	RN
Knapper, Joseph W	Able Seaman	RN

Knight, James A P	Stoker 1st Class	RN
Knight, John	Engine Room Artificer 4th Class	RN
Knight, Roy F	Midshipman	RNR
Knight, Stanley R	Joiner 4th Class	RN
Knox, John A	Ordinary Seaman	RN
Knox, John D	Stoker 2nd Class	RN

L

Ladd. Charles J	Stoker 2nd Class	RN
Laidman, Reginald A	Able Seaman	RN
Laing, John	Ordinary Seaman	RN
Laking, Andrew	Stoker 2nd Class	RN
Lambert, Thomas W	Ordinary Seaman	RN
Lancaster, Howard	Able Seaman	RN
Lane, Cyril F	Shipwright 2nd Class	RN
Lane, Herbert F W	Able Seaman	RN
Langley, James	Ordinary Coder	RN
Landsdown, Cecil R E	Canteen Assistant	NAAFI
Lapthorn, Peter R	Midshipman	RNVR
Latimer, Walter S	Ordinary Seaman	RN
Laughlin, John C A	Boy 1st Class	RN
Laws, Albert E	Chief Stoker	RN
Lawson, Jack	Cook (S)	RN
Laycock, Henry	Marine	RM
Layton, Sidney G	Marine	RM
Le Bosquet, Cecil E	Able Seaman	RN
Le Noury, Alfred N	Able Seaman	RN
Le Page, Edwin H G	Able Seaman	RN
Leach, Harold G	Mechanician 1st Class	RN
Leaney, Robert T	Boy 1st Class	RN
Leason, Harry V	Engine Room Artificer 3rd Class	RN
Lee, Wilfred	Assistant Steward	RN
Leggatt, George F S	Stoker 1st Class	RN
Leggett, Cyril A	Ordinary Seaman	RN
Leishman, William	Chief Stoker	RN
L'Enfant, Bertram H	Leading Stoker	RN
Levack, John S L	Marine	RM
Lever, Stanley R	Stoker 1st Class	RN
Levy, Albert P	Ordinary Seaman	RN
Lewington, George C	Yeoman of Signals	RN

Lewis, Alfred G	Stoker 1st Class	RN
Lewis, Edward P S	Lieutenant	RN
Lewis, Michael E	Petty Officer Stoker	RN
Lewis, Thomas	Able Seaman	RN
Liddell, Archibald T	Stoker 1st Class	RN
Liddle, Harold	Leading Seaman	RN
Lifford, henry G	Supply Assistant	RN
Lightbody, Robert	Boy 1st Class	RN
Lihou, Owen F C	Able Seaman	RN
Livingstone, Robert J	Stoker 2nd Class	RN
Lloyd, Philip	Stoker 1st Class	RN
Lock, Herbert H	Petty Officer Stoker	RN
Lock, Robert H	Marine	RM
Lockhart, Archibald W	Boy 1st Class	RN
Locklin, James	Able Seaman	RN
London, Reginald J C	Sergeant	RM
Long, George H	Musician	RM
Long, Percy CB	Boy 1st Class	RN
Lott, Frederick C	Able Seaman	RN
Love, Herbert W	Leading Stoker	RN
Lovelock, Charles W	Stoker 1st Class	RN
Lownds, John	Able Seaman	RN
Luckhurst, John H J	Able Seaman	RN
Lumley, Heaton	Major	RM
Luxmoore, Thomas G p	Lieutenant (S)	RN
Luxton, Denis W A	Engine Room Artificer 4th Class	RN
Lyle, James P	Able Seaman	RN
Lynch, Augustine P	Able Seaman	RN
Lynch, James F	Petty Officer Supply	RN

M

MacDonald, Alastair D	Boy 1st Class	RN
MacHin, John L	Lieutenant-Commander	RN
MacKay, John	Seaman	RNR
MacKin, Ronald W	Able Seaman	RN
MacLean, Hugh W P	Ordinary Coder	RN
MacNamara, Robert T	Able Seaman	RN
Madden, John F	Ordinary Seaman	RN
Maidment, Harold L	Ordinary Seaman	RN
Maitland, John W	Chief Shipwright	RN

Malcolmson, Alexander	Ordinary Seaman	RN
Malin, Walter G	Telegraphist	RN
Mann, Arthur J	Ordinary Seaman	RN
Manser, Richard A	Marine	RM
Manton, Ernest P	Cook (S)	RN
Markey, Harold E	Joiner 2nd Class	RN
Marr, Ian CC	Able Seaman	RN
Marsh, Eric	Leading Seaman	RN
Marsh, Eric	Supply Assistant	RN
Marsh, Joseph S	Able Seaman	RN
Marsh, Percy G	Marine	RM
Marsh, Robert J A	Leading Stoker	RN
Martin, John W	Boy 1st Class	RN
Martin, Thomas G	Stoker 1st Class	RN
Martin, W R	Sergeant	RM
Martindale, Norman	Boy 1st Class	RN
Maskell, John N	Able Seaman	RN
Mason, Vernon R K	Boy 1st Class	RN
Masters, Gordon H T	Boy 1st Class	RN
Matthews, Albert G	Stoker 2nd Class	RN
Matthews, Stanley G	Ordinary Telegraphist	RN
Matthews, William D	Able Seaman	RN
Maycock, Ernest V	Able Seaman	RN
McAllen, John W F	Stoker 2nd Class	RN
McAteer, William	Stoker 1st Class	RN
McCart, George	Telegraphist	RN
McCaughey, Daniel	Stoker 1st Class	RN
McCaw, Robert W	Ordinary Seaman	RN
McCleary, William	Able Seaman	RN
McCormac, John	Signal Boy	RN
McCullagh, John	Engine Room Artificer 4th Class	RN
McDonald, Ewan	Able Seaman	RN
McDonald, Harold	Able Seaman	RN
McDonald, Wallace	Able Seaman	RN
McDowell, Albert	Ordinary Seaman	RN
McDuell, Alfred	Able Seaman	RN
McEvoy, Patrick J	Able Seaman	RN
McEwan, Mark	Assistant Steward	RN
McFadyen, Walter E	Sergeant	RM
McGhee, John	Ordinary Seaman	RN
McGregor, Alfred	Stoker 1st Class	RN

McGuire, Arthur T	Chief Engine Room Artificer	RN
McIlwraith, Geoffry J	Stoker 1st Class	RN
McKim, William	Boy 1st Class	RN
McLaren, John B	Midshipman	RNR
McLatchie, William	Ordinary Seaman	RN
McLean, Alexander	Leading Stoker	RN
McLeod, Ian M	Able Seaman	RN
McNulty, John G	Chief Petty Officer Telegraphist	RN
McQuade, Ernest G	Marine	RM
McRae, William R	Boy Telegraphist	RN
Meakin, Harry	Ordinary Seaman	RN
Mellalieu, Frank	Stoker 2nd Class	RN
Melvill, John	Stoker 2nd Class	RN
Mendham, Frederick G	Boy 1st Class	RN
Mepham, Henry J	Engine Room Artificer 3rd Class	RN
Metcalfe, Matthew	Leading Seaman	RN
Middleton, Frank R	Petty Officer	RN
Milburn, Samuel C	Able Seaman	RN
Miles, Francis B	Able Seaman	RN
Miles, Ronald S	Marine	RM
Miles, Vernon G	Chief Petty Officer	RN
Millard, David T H	Able Seaman	RN
Millard, George K	Able Seaman	RN
Miller, James A K	Stoker 1st Class	RN
Miller, Thomas	Able Seaman	RN
Mills, Campbell R F	Ordinary Seaman	RN
Mills, Harry	Ordinary Seaman	RN
Mills, Montague D	Marine	RM
Mills, Raymond E	Stoker 2nd Class	RN
Mills, Ronald W	Stoker 1st Class	RN
Mitchell, Frank	Engine Room Artificer 4th Class	RN
Mitchell, Frederick R	Able Seaman	RN
Mitchell, John	Able Seaman	RN
Mitchell, Leonard F W	Able Seaman	RN
Moat, Norman	Ordinary Seaman	RN
Mochan, John C	Ordinary Seaman	RN
Monument, Harry	Joiner 4th Class	RN
Moody, Walter	Ordinary Signalman	RN
Moon, Jack E	Petty Officer	RN
Moon, Walter	Able Seaman	RN
Moore, Brian R	Ordinary Seaman	RN

Moore, Edward A P	Stoker 2nd Class	RN
Moore, Hugh T H	Petty Officer	RN
Moore, James K	Boy 1st Class	RN
Morgan, Albert H	Marine	RM
Morgan, Ronald	Marine	RM
Morley, Sidney V	Chief Petty Officer	RN
Morrell, Ronald F	Stoker 2nd Class	RN
Morten, Thomas A	Engine Room Artificer 4th Class	RN
Mortimer, Robert E G	Able Seaman	RN
Mortimer, Stanley E	Stoker 2nd Class	RN
Mould, Geoffrey J W	Able Seaman	RN
Moultrie, Edward H F	Lieutenant-Commander	RN
Mullen, John	Telegraphist	RN
Mulligan, James	Stoker 1st Class	RN
Mullins, Edgar W F	Ordinary Seaman	RN
Munday, Harold J	Wireman	RN
Murphy, Frank E	Stoker 1st Class	RN
Murray, Frederick C	Marine	RM
Murray, Hugh	Able Seaman	RN
Murray, Sidney	Electrical Artificer	RN
Murray, Thomas	Ordinary Seaman	RN
Murrel, George P	Shipwright 4th Class	RN
Myers, Gordon W	Ordinary Seaman	RN
Myers, Sidney S S	Ordinary Seaman	RN
Myram, Maurice A	Shipwright 4th Class	RN

N

Nally, Joseph	Leading Stoker	RN
Nash, Kenneth R	Stoker 1st Class	RN
Naylor, Rodney J	Chief Petty Officer Cook (O)	RN
Naylor, Ronald	Able Seaman	RN
Neal, Edward R	Supply Assistant	RN
Neal, Ronald W	Able Seaman	RN
Neale, Robert S	Marine	RM
Neave, Peter F A	Able Seaman	RN
Nelson, William	Stoker 2nd Class	RN
Nevett, Arthur L	Yeoman of Signals	RN
Neville, William A	Petty Officer	RN
Newell, Charles J	Able Seaman	RN
Newey, Cedric B N	Lieutenant	RNVR

Newnham, Robert	Able Seaman	RN
Nicholl, Donal W	Able Seaman	RN
Nicholls, Douglas H	Stoker 2nd Class	RN
Nichols, Thomas F	Ordinary Seaman	RN
Nicholson, Alfred F	Petty Officer	RN
Nicholson, Andrew	Leading Signalman	RN
Nicholson, Thomas W	Cook	RN
Noble, Alexander	Marine	RM
Norman, Christopher J B	Midshipman	RCN
Norris, Thomas F	Stoker 2nd Class	RN
Northam, William A	Able Seaman	RN
Nuding, Albert V	Supply Assistant	RN
Nugent, William J	Stoker 1st Class	RN

O

Oborne, Reginald G H	Petty Officer Steward	RN
O'Connell, John F	Petty Officer	RN
Ogden, Robert	Able Seaman	RN
Oldershaw, Arthur	Leading Stoker	RN
O'Leary, Leslie S D	Stoker 1st Class	RN
Olive, Ronald M	Cook (O)	RN
O'Neil, Owen	Ordinary Seaman	RN
O'Reilly, Dennis P	Stoker 2nd Class	RN
O'Rourke, Patrick C	Leading Seaman	RN
Orrell, Walter J	Marine	RN
Ovenden, Jack	Canteen Assistant	NAAFI
Owen, Harold	Petty Officer	RN
Owens, George E M	Lieutenant-Commander	RN

P

Pacy, Ronald	Engine Room Artificer 4th Class	RN
Paddock, Stanley A	Stoker 1st Class	RN
Pae, James	Able Seaman	RN
Page, Victor E F	Stoker 2nd Class	RN
Palmer, Frank	Stoker 1st Class	RN
Palmer, Frederick W J	Petty Officer Regulating	RN
Palmer, James A	Marine	RM
Palmer, Reginald W	Sergeant	RM
Palmer, Stephen	Able Seaman	RNVR
Papworth, Robert G	Yeoman of Signals	RN

Pares, Anthony	Lieutenant-Commander	RN
Park, Raymond	Able Seaman	RN
Parker, Gordon	Steward	RN
Parratt, Albert H	Stoker 1st Class	RN
Parton, Stanley G	Stoker 1st Class	RN
Passells, Keith C	Chief Petty Officer Supply	RN
Passey, Aubrey R	Sick Berth Attendant	RN
Patton, Owen	Able Seaman	RN
Pay, James L	Able Seaman	RN
Payne, Harry T	Able Seaman	RN
Payne, John W	Leading Stoker	RN
Peace, Denzil S	Marine	RN
Peacock, Denzil S	Surgeon-Lieutenant (D)	RN
Peacock, William	Stoker 2nd Class	RN
Pearce, Arthur S	Stoker 1st Class	RN
Pearce, Harry R	Engine Room Artificer 3rd Class	RN
Pearce, Ronald J	Leading Supply Assistant	RN
Pearce, William F	Petty Officer	RN
Pearse, Jon F F	Electrical Artificer 1st Class	RN
Pearse, Sidney C	Able Seaman	RN
Pearson, George	Cook (O)	RN
Peck, Owen O	Able Seaman	RN
Peckham, Leonard M	Ordinary Seaman	RN
Pedder, Ernest A J	Able Seaman	RN
Peden, David G	Ordinary Seaman	RN
Peel, Reginald K	Assistant Steward	RN
Peirce, James P	Chief Petty Officer Steward	RN
Pemberon, Frederick S	Engine Room Artificer 4th Class	RN
Pennycook, William R	Stoker 2nd Class	RN
Percival, Stanley E P	Stoker 2nd Class	RN
Perkins, William G	Marine	RM
Perman, Roland G C	Midshipman	RIN
Perrin, Alfred J	Cook (S)	RN
Perry, Aubrey J W	Steward	RN
Perry, Leonard	Marine	RM
Perry, William H	Petty Officer Cook(O)	RN
Pescod, Thomas C	Boy 1st Class	RN
Petch, Roy V	Able Seaman	RN
Petty, Edmund J	Able Seaman	RN
Phelps, Henry F	Blacksmith 1st Class	RN
Phillips, George T E	Ordinary Seaman	RN

Phillips, Horace E	Leading Seaman	RN
Phillips, Lancelot J	Ordinary Seaman	RN
Phillips, Norman	Stoker 2nd Class	RN
Phillips, Raymond T	Ordinary Seaman	RN
Phillips, Ronald G	Paymaster Lieutenant (S)	RN
Pickering, Harry	Petty Officer Stoker	RN
Pierce, Robert D	Marine	RM
Pike, William A	Musician	RM
Pink, Harold J	Able Seaman	RN
Pinkerton, Robert	Wireman	RN
Piper, Fred H	Ordinary Signalman	RNVR
Pitts, Henry G	Ordinary Seaman	RN
Plant, Edwin	Marine	RM
Plimbley, Edward C	Leading Steward	RN
Plumley, Reginald A H	Warrant Engineer	RN
Poar, Reginald J	Marine	RM
Pope, Geoffrey C	Chief Petty Officer Supply	RN
Porter, Cyril L D	Ordinary Signalman	RN
Porter, Frederick A	Marine	RM
Porter, Reginald J	Musician	RM
Porter-Fausset, Frederick A P		
	Lieutenant (S)	RN
Potts, Frank S	Writer	RN
Power, Alfred	Able Seaman	RN
Powley, Herbert W	Chief Engine Room Artificer	RN
Prangnell, Maurice R	Able Seaman	RN
Pratt, Albert W C	Marine	RM
Prescott, Marcus R	Petty Officer Stoker	RN
Price, Alfred C J P	Shipwright 4th Class	RN
Price, William A	Warrant Shipwright	RN
Pringle, Robert H W	Stoker 1st Class	RN
Print, Dennis C B	Engine Room Artificer 4th Class	RN
Proudlock, Eric	Able Seaman	RN
Pulling, Edward	Petty Officer Stoker	RN
Punter, Jack A	Able Seaman	RN
Puttick, William F	Stoker 1st Class	RN
Puttock, Maurice J E	Signalman	RNVR

Q

Quigly, John J	Ordinary Seaman	RN

R

Radley, Kenneth	Stoker 1st Class	RN
Rae, Hector R	Plumber 3rd Class	RN
Ramsbottom, Leonard	Shipwright 4th Class	RN
Rance, John	Leading Stoker	RN
Randall, Cyril W	Able Seaman	RN
Randall, Maurice P	Boy 1st Class	RN
Randall, Stanley	Marine	RM
Randall, Victor J	Stoker 1st Class	RN
Rant, Leonard	Stoker 2nd Class	RN
Raw, Dennis A	Engine Room Artificer 4th Class	RN
Raw, Irving T	Able Seaman	RN
Raw, Roderick M	Stoker 1st Class	RN
Rawlinson, Albert G E	Stoker 1st Class	RN
Rawlinson, Leonard	Able Seaman	RN
Raynor, Francis	Signalman	RN
Read, Anthony V	Ordinary Seaman	RN
Read, Douglas	Boy 1st Class	RN
Reay, William E	Petty Officer	RN
Reddall, Peter E A	Signal Boy	RN
Reed, Hector L	Corporal	RM
Rees, Vernon J	Stoker 1st Class	RN
Reeve, Robert E	Leading Steward	RN
Reeves, Cyril A	Able Seaman	RN
Reeves, Stanley E	Ordinary Seaman	RN
Rendell, Stewart R J	Able Seaman	RN
Reveler, Thomas S	Engine Room Artificer 4th Class	RN
Reynolds, John A	Stoker 2nd Class	RN
Rhodes, John	Steward	RN
Rice, Herbert F	Stoker 2nd Class	RN
Richards, Alfred W	Stoker 1st Class	RN
Richardson, Henry F D	Ordinary Signalman	RN
Richardson, Snowden F O	Stoker 1st Class	RN
Richer, Harold E	Petty Officer	RN
Ridfe, Merlin F	Writer	RN
Riding, Walter K	Ordinary Seaman	RN
Rigby, Benjamin G	Boy 1st Class	RN
Rigglesford, Arthur P	Stoker 1st Class	RN
Riley, George P	Stoker 1st Class	RN
Ritchie, James S	Petty Officer Telegraphist	RN

Ritchie, Thomas B	Electrical Artificer 4th Class	RN
Roach, Bryan C J	Lieutenant (E)	RN
Robarts, Frederick J	Ordinary Telegraphist	RN
Robb, James G	Able Seaman	RN
Robbins, Robert S	Ordinary Seaman	RN
Roberts, Ernest G	Mechanician 2nd Class	RN
Roberts, Frederick C	Leading Seaman	RN
Roberts, Gordon R	Able Seaman	RN
Roberts, Lewis G	Able Seaman	RN
Roberts, Reginald C	Ordinary Seaman	RN
Robins, Anthony C R	Sub-Lieutenant	RNR
Robins, Charles V	Yeoman of Signals	RN
Robinson, Arthur E	Able Seaman	RN
Robinson, Percival T	Petty Officer Cook	RN
Robinson, Peter J	Boy 1st Class	RN
Robotham, Charles	Able Seaman	RN
Rodgman, Claude B	Able Seaman	RN
Rodley, Samuel J	Marine	RM
Roe, Donovan C	Commander (S)	RN
Rooney, John P	Seaman	RNR
Rootham, Peter	Ordinary Seaman	RN
Rorrison, Hugh F	Boy 1st Class	RN
Rose, Reginald T	Stoker 1st Class	RN
Rose, William J	Stoker 2nd Class	RN
Rosenthal, Henry C	Marine	RM
Routledge, Walter	Boy 1st Class	RN
Rowe, Stanley G S	Marine	RM
Rowlands, Daniel J	Marine	RM
Rowntree, George W	Stoker 1st Class	RN
Rowsell, Graham H	Able Seaman	RN
Rowsell, Leslie D	Boy 1st Class	RN
Roy. Ian E	Boy 1st Class	RN
Rudd, Edwin A	Ordnance Artificer 4th Class	RN
Rundle, Arthur F	Marine	RM
Runnacles, Frederick E	Marine	RM
Russell, Charles A	Able Seaman	RN
Russell, David L	Musician	RM
Russell, John A G	Petty Officer	RN
Russell, Leonard W	Able Seaman	RN
Russell, Walter F	Petty Officer	RN
Ryder, Leonard	Petty Officer Telegraphist	RN

S

Sadler, Edward R	Marine	RM
Saiger, John G	Stoker 1st Class	RN
Sammars, Thomas J B	Boy 1st Class	RN
Sanderson, Peter	Able Seaman	RN
Sargeaunt, Henry E J	Stoker 2nd Class	RN
Saul, Charles	Leading Stoker	RN
Saunders, Albert	Marine	RM
Saunders, Arthur W	Engine Room Artificer 4th Class	RN
Saunders, James G	Stoker 2nd Class	RN
Savage, Edwin J	Chief Engine Room Artificer	RN
Sayers, Robert M	Ordinary Seaman	RN
Scammell, Walter G	Leading Stoker	RN
Scattergood, Frederick J	Stoker 1st Class	RN
Scott, Andrew B	Seaman	RN
Scott, Jack	Ordinary Seaman	RN
Scott, James	Leading Stoker	RN
Scott, Robert C	Marine	RM
Scott, William P	Stoker 2nd Class	RN
Scott-Kerr,John A A	Sub-Lieutenant	RN
Senior, Reuben	Stoker 2nd Class	RN
Sewell, Gilbert W	Marine	RM
Shadbolt, Maurice H	Marine	RM
Shand, Robert	Able Seaman	RN
Shannon, John D	Ordinary Seaman	RAN
Sharp, John S	Steward	RN
Sharpe, Albert J	Stoker 2nd Class	RN
Shawe, Robert B	Able Seaman	RN
Shearer, George B B	Leading Cook (S)	RN
Shepherd, Cyril H	Ordinary Seaman	RN
Shepherd, George V	Engine Room Artificer	RN
Shepherd, Lambert C	Ordinary Seaman	RN
Shepherd, Percy R	Able Seaman	RN
Sheppard, Leonard F G	Petty Officer	RN
Sherval, William R	Chief Stoker	RN
Shiers, William H	Petty Officer Supply	RN
Shipp, Leslie F	Stoker 1st Class	RN
Shorrock, Stanley HA	Able Seaman	RN
Short, Arthur E	Engine Room Artificer 4th Class	RN
Shuck, William B	Ordnance Artificer 5th Class	RN

Shuker, McHibald	Leading Seaman	RN
Shute, Harry L	Leading Cook (O)	RN
Siddall, John	Able Seaman	RN
Sidley, Robert B P	Petty Officer Stoker	RN
Silk, Jack C R	Stoker 2nd Class	RN
Sim, Alexander E	Sick Berth Attendant	RN
Simmons, Ernest A	Stoker 1st Class	RN
Simpson, Peter	Ordinary Seaman	RN
Sims, William	Engine Room Artificer 4th Class	RN
Sinnott, Frederick W	Able Seaman	RN
Skett, Raymond L	Ordnance Artificer 4th Class	RN
Skipper, John F	Able Seaman	RN
Slade, Ronald A	Able Seaman	RN
Slowther, George	Petty Officer Stoker	RN
Smart, Leslie E V	Able Seaman	RN
Smith, Alexander G	Steward	RN
Smith, Andrew K	Able Seaman	RN
Smith, Benjamin T	Marine	RM
Smith, Charles L S	Able Seaman	RN
Smith, Dick	Able Seaman	RN
Smith, Eric T	Ordinary Seaman	RN
Smith, Frederick A	Able Seaman	RN
Smith, Frederick H S	Petty Officer Stoker	RN
Smith, George F	Stoker 1st Class	RN
Smith, Harold G E	Lieutenant (E)	RN
Smith, James	Able Seaman	RN
Smith, James M	Able Seaman	RN
Smith, John C	Ordinary Seaman	RN
Smith, John H	Chief Petty Officer	RN
Smith, John H	Petty Officer Regulating	RN
Smith, John H	Supply Assistant	RN
Smith, Peter W C	Supply Assistant	RN
Smith, Stanley C	Leading Cook	RN
Smith, Stephen R	Able Seaman	RN
Smith, Thomas	Ordinary Seaman	RN
Smith, Thomas N	Stoker 1st Class	RN
Smith, Walter H	Leading Seaman	RN
Smith, William G	Able Seaman	RN
Smith-Withers, Stephen J	Wireman	RN
Snelgrove, Colin	Leading Seaman	RN
Snell, John	Chief Engine Room Artificer	RN

Snook, George A	Marine	RM
Snooks, William H	Ordinary Seaman	RN
Snow, David J	Boy 1st Class	RN
Solmon, Murdoch M	Able Seaman	RN
Southgate, Thomas E	Marine	RM
Sowerby, Curzon	Writer	RN
Sparkes, Ernest	Marine	RM
Spence, Tristram F	Lieutenant (E)	RN
Spencer, Arthur	Mechanician 2nd Class	RN
Spinner, George D	Stoker 1st Class	RN
Sprakes, John	Chief Stoker	RN
Spreadbury, Jack F W	Ordinary Seaman	RN
St Clair-Tracy, Albert E	Electrical Artificer 2nd Class	RN
Stanley, Leonard	Able Seaman	RN
Stannard, George W	Petty Officer Sick Berth	RN
Startup, Ian G E	Ordinary Seaman	RANVR
Steel, Douglas M	Commander (Instructor)	RN
Steele, Alexander	Able Seaman	RN
Steele, Joseph W	Ordinary Seaman	RN
Steptoe, John H	Marine	RM
Steven, Arthur	Petty Officer Stoker	RN
Stevenson, Basil P	Midshipman	RNR
Stevenson, Noel	Ordnance Artificer 5th Class	RN
Stewart, Albert M	Able Seaman	RN
Stewart, Robert J	Chaplain	RN
Stewart, Thomas	Able Seaman	RN
Stibbs, Charles T	Ordinary Seaman	RN
Stocker, Norman G L	Boy 1st Class	RN
Stoddard, George H P	Marine	RM
Stokes, John E	Able Seaman	RN
Stone, Arthur W	Petty Officer	RN
Stothers, Hugh	Able Seaman	RN
Stoyles, Sydney S	Chief Stoker	RN
Strange, Edward J	Stoker 1st Class	RN
Strerne, Benjamin S	Able Seaman	RN
Stringer, Cecil A B	Able Seaman	RN
Strong, Arthur	Leading Writer	RN
Stubbings, Douglas H	Marine	RM
Stubbs, Charles F B	Lieutenant	RNVR
Sturgess, Cyril L	Able Seaman	RN
Sturgess, John P	Boy 1st Class	RN

Sulley, John C	Commissioned Ordnance Officer	RN
Sullivan, Albert	Petty Officer Stoker	RN
Sullivan, Frank D	Stoker 2nd Class	RN
Surrey, Archibald H	Chief Petty Officer Writer	RN
Swain, James F	Leading Writer	RN
Swain, Ronald W	Ordinary Telegraphist	RN
Swanborough, Rupert T	Cook (O)	RN
Swatton, Bertram C	Petty Officer	RN
Swinson, Ernest J	Ordnance Artificer 3rd Class	RN
Switzer, Albert	Ordinary Seaman	RN
Sylvester, James	Ordinary Telegraphist	RN
Symes, Reginald C	Wireman	RN
Szymalski, K	Midshipman	PN

T

Taggart, Robert	Assistant Cook (S)	RN
Tallett, Ronald L W	Leading Seaman	RN
Tamarelle, Michael	Electrical Artificer 4th Class	RN
Tapsell, Albert E	Marine	RM
Tawney, David R	Musician	RM
Taylor, Arnold E	Ordinary Seaman	RN
Taylor, Charles	Leading Seaman	RN
Taylor, Charles A	Telegraphist	RN
Taylor, Clifford	Leading Stoker	RN
Taylor, David	Wireman	RN
Taylor, Frederick	Able Seaman	RN
Taylor, Henry C	Stoker 1st Class	RN
Taylor, James	Stoker 2nd Class	RN
Taylor, Lewis J	Marine	RM
Taylor, Reginald L	Musician	RM
Taylor, William C	Ordinary Telegraphist	RN
Taylor, William O	Commissioned Telegraphist	RN
Telford, Charles	Marine	RM
Terry, Gordon V	Telegraphist	RN
Thomas, Francis J	Able Seaman	RN
Thomas, Harold J	Able Seaman	RN
Thompson, Harold	Able Seaman	RN
Thompson, Robert	Boy 1st Class	RN
Thomson, Hugh	Able Seaman	RN
Thorpe, George E	Leading Stoker	RN

Thorpe, Joseph	Marine	RM
Thorpe, Richard	Ordinary Seaman	RN
Thurogood, John F	Cook (S)	RN
Till, Jack C	Telegraphist	RN
Till, William E C	Shipwright	RN
Tipping, Alfred J E	Able Seaman	RN
Titheridge, Jack R	Canteen Assistant	NAAFI
Tocher, Edwin	Ordinary Seaman	RN
Todd, William C	Stoker 1st Class	RN
Tomlins, George	Leading Seaman	RN
Tomlinson, William T	Boy 1st Class	RN
Toogood, Leslie B	Marine	RM
Topham, Thomas	Able Seaman	RN
Townley, William J	Stoker 2nd Class	RN
Tozer, Harry G H	Commissioned Gunner	RN
Treloar, Walter J B	Leading Seaman	RN
Trevarthen, William	Canteen Manager	NAAFI
Trollope, Clifton W	Stoker 2nd Class	RN
Trotter, Ralph W	Petty Officer Telegraphist	RN
Trowbridge, William C	Petty Officer	RN
Tucker, Leslie	Ordinary Seaman	RN
Turnbull, William S	Able Seaman	RN
Turner, George F	Stoker 1st Class	RN
Turner, George H F	Stoker 1st Class	RN
Turner, John	Stoker 1st Class	RN
Tuxworth, Frank A	Ordinary Signalman	RN
Twigg, Charles J	Stoker 1st Class	RN

U

Underwood, John	Stoker 2nd Class	RN
Upton, Roy R	Ordinary Telegraphist	RN
Utteridge, Raymond H	Petty Officer Telegraphist	RN

V

Vacher, Geoffrey D B	Midshipman (S)	RN
Varlow, Albert C M	Commissioned Gunner	RN
Varndell, Arthur G	Petty Officer Stoker	RN
Veal, Richard E	Chief Petty Officer Cook	RN
Vickers, Herbert G	Chief Petty Officer	RN
Viney, Albert E	Marine	RM

W

Wagstaff, William	Able Seaman	RN
Walker, Albert	Petty Officer	RN
Walker, George	Ordinary Signalman	RN
Walker, Thomas	Stoker 1st Class	RN
Wallace, James W	Leading Stoker	RN
Waller, William J	Stoker 2nd Class	RN
Wallis, Michael H S J	Marine	RM
Walsh, John F	Assistant Cook (S)	RN
Walter, William F P	Warrant Engineer	RN
Walters, Douglas T	Assistant Cook (S)	RN
Walton, Clifford	Marine	RM
Walton, John	Leading Seaman	RN
Walton, Josiah T	Chief Stoker	RN
Wannerton, Henry J	Leading Stoker	RN
Ward, Frederick W	Painter 3rd Class	RN
Ward, George	Signalman	RN
Ward, Joseph	Ordinary Telegraphist	RN
Warden, Kenneth G	Midshipman	RNR
Warrand, Selwyn J P	Commander	RN
Warren, Donald	Marine	RM
Warwick, Benjamin	Boy 1st Class	RN
Waterhouse, Reginald G	Able Seaman	RN
Waterlow, Antony A	Ordinary Signalman	RN
Waterman, Albert D	Able Seaman	RN
Waters, William F	Stoker 1st Class	RN
Waterson, Thomas J B	Leading Stoker	RN
Watkins, John	Petty Officer Stoker	RN
Watkinson, Stanley	Paymaster Sub-Lieutenant	RNZN
Watson, Alexander	Seaman	RNR
Watson, John C	Able Seaman	RN
Watson, Robert	Able Seaman	RN
Watson, Harry	Chief Stoker	RN
Watt, Charles J J	Stoker 1st Class	RN
Watt, Robert E	Steward	RN
Watts, Edward A H	Chief Petty Officer	RN
Watts, Henry A	Ordinary Telegraphist	RN
Wearn, Arthur	Marine	RM
Wearne, Harry E	Able Seaman	RN
Weaver, Henry E	Marine	RM

Webb, Albert	Able Seaman	RN
Weddle, William	Able Seaman	RN
Welch, Albert C W	Stoker 1st Class	RN
Welch, Reginald A	Petty Officer	RN
Welch, Sidney C T	Marine	RM
Weldon, Eric	Able Seaman	RN
Welman, Arthur C	Petty Officer Stoker	RN
Wells, Henry	Stoker 2nd Class	RN
Wells, Herbert W	Ordinary Seaman	RN
Wells, Horace W	Stoker 1st Class	RN
Wells, Philip J	Corporal	RM
Wells, Ronald D G	Able Seaman	RN
Wells, Stanley	Boy 1st Class	RN
West, Alfred P	Petty Officer Cook (S)	RN
West, Robert W	Chief Engine Room Artificer	RN
Wharfe, Cyril P	Petty Officer	RN
Wheeler, Ernest F	Gunner	RN
Wheeler, Francis W	Able Seaman	RN
White, Arthur	Wireman	RN
White, Edward H	Petty Officer Telegraphist	RN
White, Harry	Marine	RM
Whitehead, Reginald C	Sergeant	RM
Whireman, John W	Petty Officer Stoker	RN
Whitewood, Cyril J	Able Seaman	RN
Whitfield, Victor V	Petty Officer	RN
Wicks, Hubert G	Able Seaman	RN
Wigfall, Leslie A	Engine Room Artificer 3rd Class	RN
Wiggett, James K	Stoker 2nd Class	RN
Wigzell, Norman F H	Ordinary Coder	RN
Wilcocks, Eric C	Able Seaman	RN
Wilcockson, Harry R	Stoker 1st Class	RN
Wilkins, George H	Able Seaman	RN
Wilkinson, Frederick J R	Boy 1st Class	RN
Wilkinson, James W	Stoker 1st Class	RN
Wilkinson, Stanley	Leading Seaman	RN
Willets, Tom	Sub-Lieutenant	RNVR
Williams, Frederick P	Ordinary Seaman	RN
Williams, Horace A	Painter 3rd Class	RN
Williams, Leonard J	Able Seaman	RN
Williams, Lloyd	Electrical Artificer 4th Class	RN
Williams, Roderick G	Midshipman	RNVR

Williams, Roland M	Writer	RN
Williams, Tom G J	Able Seaman	RN
Williamson, Harry	Leading Stoker	RN
Willis, Albert	Stoker 1st Class	RN
Wilmhurst, George H	Leading Seaman	RN
Wilson, Gordon A C	Able Seaman	RN
Wilson, George	Able Seaman	RN
Wilson, Herbert G	Leading Seaman	RN
Wilson, John V	Ordinary Seaman	RN
Wilson, Walter	Signalman	RN
Windeatt, Ralph F	Boy Telegraphist	RN
Wingfield, Charles H	Petty Officer Cook (S)	RN
Winkfield, Victor M	Leading Stoker	RN
Wishart, Jack E	Marine	RM
Woelfell, Edward J E	Writer	RN
Wood, William E	Able Seaman	RN
Woodward, Frederick J	Warrant Electrician	RN
Wootton, Desmond T	Boy 1st Class	RN
Worboys, Robert M	Stoker 1st Class	RN
Worrall, Arthur	Stoker 2nd Class	RN
Worsfold, Sydney G	Band Corporal	RM
Worwood, Raymond F	Able Seaman	RN
Wright, Alfred W	Ordinary Seaman	RN
Wright, Charles E	Petty Officer Telegraphist	RN
Wright, George	Yeoman of Signals	RN
Wright, Stanley W F	Supply Assistant	RN
Wright, Thomas C	Leading Seaman	RN
Wrighting, Douglas H W	Stoker 2nd Class	RN
Wyatt, Jeffrey A F	Marine	RM
Wyldbore-Smith, Hugh D	Lieutenant-Commander	RN

Y

Yarrow, Peter M	Ordinary Seaman	RN
Yates, Robert G	Boatswain	RN
Young, John O	Signalman	RN
Young, Percy A	Boy Bugler	RM
Younger, Albert	Marine	RM

Z

Zmud-Trzebiatowski, L	Midshipman	PN
Zurek, O	Midshipman	PN

Memorial Gallery

Victor E Adams
Ordinary Seaman   Age 19

Alfred K Algate
Canteen Assistant ((NAAFI))

Harry C Alland
Petty Officer

George Allott
Marine

Arthur D Anderson
Able Seaman   Age 18

James E Annis
Stoker 1st Class   Age 21

William A Arnold
Petty Officer Stoker   Age 29

Albert GL Austin
Able Seaman   Age 20

Frank R Ayling
Canteen Assistant (NAAFI)

Henry D Ayres
Ordinary Signalman   Age 18

Kenneth A Baker
Petty Officer Telegraphist   Age 42

Percy H Balch
Able Seaman   Age 31

Philip A Ball
Stoker 1st Class

Arthur C Barclay
Leading Cook   Age 20

Thomas Barker
Ordinary Seaman   Age 18

Geoffrey V Beardsley
Joiner 4th Class

James R Belsham
Able Seaman

Ernest FT Benwell
Chief Petty Officer, Sick Berth   Age

Walden J Biggenden
Chief Stoker   Age 52

Herbert G A Bird
Ordinance Officer 3rd Class

Charles J Bishop
Chief Stoker

Edward J P Bishop
Petty Officer

Arthur B Bleach
Able Seaman

Stanley Boardman
Petty Officer

William L Boncey
Petty Officer

Jack Boniface
Able Seaman

Norman Boneham
Marine

Leo S Bowers
Ordinary Seaman

Arthur W Brewer
Ordinary Seaman, brother of George
Brewer also lost

George Brewer
Ordinary Seaman, brother of Willia
Brewer also lost.

Kenneth C Bridges
Ordinary Telegraphist   Age 26

Gordon B Brooks
Stoker 1st Class   Age 20

George W Broom
Shipwright 3rd Class   Age 29

Robert K Brown
Petty Officer Stoker

Arthur EJ Buck
Mechanician 2nd Class   Age 32

Herbert TJ Buck
Petty Officer Stoker   Age 29

Philip J Buckett
Midshipman

Henry W Bullock
Marine   Age 31

Kenneth F Bullman
Petty Officer

Robert H Burkin
Marine

Harry F Bussey
Able Seaman   Age 41

Arthur T Carey
Ordinary Seaman   Age 18

Robert Carter
Marine

Alfred J Chandler
Master at Arms　Age 41

Leslie H Clarke
Electrical Artificer 4th Class　Age 27

Alfred J Cockhead
Leading Stoker　Age 37

Thomas E Cogger
Marine　Age 39

William A Compton
Leading Stoker

James Cook
Chief Stoker

Frederick GD Cooper
Mechanician 2nd Class   Age 28

Harold L Cordell
Chief Petty Officer   Age 34

John Corlett
Engine Room Artificer 4th Class Age

John Coulson
Musician   Age 30

Aylmer NJ Cranston
Stoker 1st Class

Lawrence Crawley
Stoker 1st Class   Age 30

Henry R Cresswell
Marine   Age 24

Lambert E Croucher
Able Seaman

Stanislaw Czerny
Midshipman (Polish Navy)   Age 21

Richard H Dale
Lieutenant (E)

Hamilton K Davies
Midshipman   Age 19

Herbert A Davis
Marine   Age 38

Cyril AJ Dean
Stoker 1st Class

Martin Dempsey
Able Seaman

Nicholas Dobeson
Chief Petty Officer   Age 44

William F Dowdell
Leading Seaman

Ernest Drury
Ordinary Signalman   Age 18

Stephen E Dunn
Able Seaman   Age 19

Frank A Erridge
Telegraphist   Age 20

Clifford Farrar
Marine   Age 21

Leslie J Foden
Leading Seaman   Age 32

Rodney A Foley
Chief Stoker   Age 40

Jack Ford
Able Seaman   Age 18

Harold E Ford
Ordinary Seaman

Victor Forrest
Petty Officer Steward   Age 21

Ralph Foster
Ordinary Seaman   Age 25

George Fotheringham
Marine

Neville H Frodsham
Acting Sub-Lieutenant   Age 20

Joseph Gallant
Ordinary Seaman

William Gallant
Ordinary Seaman

Howard W Galliott
Ordinary Seaman　Age 22

Thomas K Gascoine
Able Seaman　Age 22

Samuel Gaudet
Ordinary Seaman

John H Gibson
Signalman

George P Gillett
Ordinary Seaman　Age 24

John R Gillis
Ordinary Seaman   Age 26

Robert Glenn
Petty Officer Stoker   Age 32

Bernard EC Good
Marine   Age 23

Alan E Hadley
Ordinary Seaman   Age 18

John S Harding
Able Seaman   Age 17

Charles A Harris
Chief Mechanician   Age 39

James H Harris
Marine

Ronald Henshaw
Boy 1st Class

Ronald Hives
Stoker 1st Class

Frederick J Hobbs
Chief Stoker

Lancelot E Holland, CB
Vice-Admiral   Age 52

Arthur Holroyd
Sailmaker's Mate   Age 23

Richard J Honeybun
Chief Stoker

Eric S Howard
Ordinary Seaman

Reginald E Howe
Stoker 2nd Class   Age 23

Gordon Hows
Marine   Age 20

Henry F Huntley
Plumber 1st Class   Age 36

John M Iago
Lieutenant (E)   Age 25

Frederick Johnson
Leading Cook   Age 28

James Johnston
Able Seaman   Age 25

Harold H Jones
Able Seaman   Age 20

Geoffrey W Jordan
Canteen Assistant ((NAAFI))Age 18

Alexander Kerr
Engine Room Artificer

Ralph Kerr CBE
Captain   Age 49

267

John Knight
Engine Room Artificer 4th Class Age 22

John Knox
Ordinary Seaman

Cyril F Lane
Shipwright 2nd Class   Age 29

Cecil RE Lansdowne
Canteen Assistant ((NAAFI))

Peter R Lapthorn
Midshipman   Age 20

Harold G Leach
Mechanician 1st Class   Age 33

George FS Leggatt
Stoker 1st Class   Age 20

Owen FC Lihou
Able Seaman   Age 20

Herbert E Lovegrove
Leading Gunner 1st Class   Age 24

Heaton Lumley
Major (Royal Marines)

John WF McAllen
Stoker 2nd Class

Ewen McDonald
Able Seaman   Age 21

Albert McDowell
Ordinary Seaman   Age 18

Alfred McDuell
Able Seaman   Age 24

Patrick J McEvoy
Able Seaman   Age 19

Mark McEwan
Assistant Steward   Age 24

John MacKay
Seaman   Age 21

Alexander Malcolmson
Ordinary Seaman   Age 23

Richard A Manser
Jr.Marine   Age 29

Ernest P Manton
Cook (S)   Age 28

Vernon R Mason
Boy 1st Class   Age 18

Henry J Mepham
Engine Room Artificer 3rd Class Age 32

Samuel C Milburn
Able Seaman

Ronald S Miles
Marine

Ronald W Mills
Stoker 1st Class   Age 22

Geoffrey J W Mould
Able Seaman   Age 18

Edward H F Moultrie
Lieutenant-Commander

Maurice A Myram
Shipwright 4th Class   Age 22

Kenneth R Nash
Stoker 1st Class   Age 21

Rodney J Naylor
Petty Officer Cook (O)   Age 39

William Nelson
Stoker 2nd Class

Arthur L Nevett
Yeoman of Signals

Jack Ovenden
Canteen Assistant((NAAFI))   Age 17

Reginald W Palmer
Sergeant   Age 28

Robert G Papwoth
Yeoman of Signals   Age 23

Keith C Passells
Chief Petty Officer Supply   Age 36

Owen Patton
Able Seaman   Age 23

John W Payne
Leading Stoker   Age 35

Owen O'R Peck
Able Seaman

William G Perkins
Marine   Age 19

Raymond T Phillips
Ordinary Seaman

Harold J Pink
Able Seaman Age 20

Reginald Plumley
Warrant Engineer

Reginald J Poar
Marine

Geoffrey C Pope
Chief Petty Officer Supply

Maurice G Prangnell
Able Seaman   Age 21

William A Price
Warrant Shipwright   Age 41

Cyril W Randall
Able Seaman   Age 18

Hector R Rae
Plumber 3rd Class   Age 27

Robert E Reeve
Leading Steward   Age 40

Stanley E Reeves
Ordinary Seaman

Stewart RJ Rendell
Able Seaman   Age 19

Walter K Riding
Ordinary Seaman   Age 18

James G Robb
Able Seaman

Lewis G Roberts
Able Seaman   Age 22

Reginald C Roberts
Ordinary Seaman

Charles V Robins
Yeoman of Signals   Age 22

Peter Rootham
Ordinary Seaman

Leslie D Rowsell
Boy 1st Class   Age 17

Leonard Ryder
Petty Officer Telegraphist   Age 37

Edward R Sadler
Marine

Cyril H Shepherd
Ordinary Seaman   Age 18

George V Shepherd
Chief Engine Room Artificer   Age 36

Percy R Shepherd
Able Seaman   Age 24

Harry L Shute
Leading Cook (O)   Age 39

Alexander E Sim
Sick Berth Attendant

George Slowther
Petty Officer Stoker

Leslie E V Smart
Able Seaman   Age 18

Eric T Smith
Ordinary Seaman   Age 30

Thomas N Smith
Stoker 1st Class

William H Snooks
Ordinary Seaman   Age 20

Ernest Sparkes
Marine   Age 19

Jack FW Spreadbury
Ordinary Seaman

Arthur Steven
Petty Officer Stoker   Age 40

Charles T Stibbs
Ordinary Seaman   Age 26

Arthur J Strong
Leading Writer   Age 23

John C Sulley
Commissioned Ordinance Officer Age 45

Frank D Sullivan
Stoker 2nd Class

Rupert T Swanborough
Cook (O) Age 21

Kazimierz Szymalski
Midshipman (Polish Navy)Age 20

Reginald L Taylor
Musician

Robert Thompson
Boy 1st Class

William EC Till
Shipwright 3rd Class

William Trevarthen
Canteen Manager ((NAAFI))   Age 46

Albert E St. C.-Tracy
Electrical Artificer

Trzebiatowski-Zmuda
Midshipman (Polish Navy)   Age 2

Frank A Tuxworth
Ordinary Signalman   Age 20

Richard Veal
Chief Petty Officer Cook

William Wagstaff
Able Seaman

John Walton
Leading Seaman   Age 23

Henry J Wannerton
Leading Stoker   Age 37

Frederick W Ward
Painter 3rd Class   Age 28

John Warrand
Commander

Harry Watson BEM
Chief Stoker   Age 37

Ronald DG Wells
Able Seaman

Robert W West
Chief Engine Room Artificer   Age 39

Harry White
Marine   Age 18

Reginald C Whitehead
Sergeant   Age 26

Cyril J Whitehead
Able Seaman

Eric C Wilcocks
Able SeamanAge 19

Lloyd Williams
Electrical Artificer 4th Class   Age 22

Harry Williamson
Able Seaman   Age 23

Charles H Wingfield
Petty Officer Cook (S)

Frederick J Woodward
Warrant Electrician

Robert M Worboys
Stoker 1st Class   Age 20

Charles E Wright
Petty Officer Telegraphist   Age 25

Hugh Wyldbore-Smith
Lieutenant-Commander   Age 34

Kazimierz Zurek
Midshipman (Polish Navy)   Age 22

'Eternal Father strong to save,
Whose arm doth bind the restless wave,
Who bidd'st the mighty ocean deep
Its own appointed limits keep;
O hear us as we cry to thee
For those in peril on the sea.'